*To Tom —
Great to meet
Mah Agee*
Karla

THE
Agile-Minded
EXECUTIVE

Drive Better Results by Shifting How You Think

Karla Robertson

 INDIE BOOKS
INTERNATIONAL

ISBN: 1-941870-21-X
ISBN 13: 978-1-941870-21-1
Library of Congress Control Number: 2015936215

Designed by Joni McPherson, mcphersongraphics.com

INDIE BOOKS INTERNATIONAL, LLC
2424 VISTA WAY, SUITE 316
OCEANSIDE, CA 92054
www.indiebooksintl.com

To Mom and Dad, the source of all that is good in me

To Linda, my sister with whom I share laughter, mischief and abiding love—always have, always will

CONTENTS

Preface   vii

Section One: Why Take the Journey?   1

Chapter 1: Tommy's Story: An Airman's
    Mind Shift Saga   3

Chapter 2: Why Do You Need an Agile Mind?   15
  • A Few Key Points About the Human Brain

Section Two: The Road Trip to Building Agility   35

Chapter 3: Getting Ready to Take the Trip   37
  • Warming Up the Engine   37
  • Pick A Lane   39
  • Know Your Destination—The Big Picture   41
  • You Are Here   43
  • Pick Your Passengers Well   45

Chapter 4: Hazards on the Road   49
  • Encountering Stormy Conditions   49
  • Detours-Welcome Them   52
  • Limitations: Six-Lane Traffic on a Two-Lane Road   55
  • Dealing with Roadblocks   59
  • Warning: Hazardous Silence Ahead   63
  • Are We There Yet?—Complaining: The Strain on
    Your Brain   68
  • Dealing With Unruly Passengers   75
  • When Darkness Sets In   81
  • Potholes, Flat Tires and Running Out of Gas   87

Chapter 5: Veering Off Course and Finding Your
    Way Back   **91**
    • It's OK To Be Lost   **91**
    • Wrong Way? Mistakes Are Your Friend   **94**
    • Knowing When to Take the Next Exit   **99**

Section Three: The Drive for Better Results Never Ends   **105**

Chapter 6: Lessons from the Road   **107**
    • You Are There   **107**
    • I.D.E.A.   **109**

Chapter 7: Afterword   **115**

Appendix A: About the Author   **121**

Appendix B: Acknowledgments   **123**

Appendix C: Services Available   **129**

Appendix D: Resources   **131**

Index   **133**

PREFACE

My purpose in writing this book is to invite people to become better thinkers in order to drive better outcomes. The genesis of becoming a better thinker lies in the mindful internal shifts we make to combine and synthesize what our emotions and logic—our whole brain—provide us. From the standpoint of executive leadership and overall business performance, I think this is becoming more and more relevant and in demand for people in executive roles. The volatile and complex challenges and opportunities we all face require us to adapt our minds to the shifting landscape developing a more nimble approach to assessing the situation and crafting solutions while keeping ourselves and each other in tact. Executives need to make tough decisions and certainly they will not please everyone. Along the way to coming to a decision, we need to open up the way we think. How we choose to think about the circumstances in which we find ourselves determines largely our level of success in dealing with them—more so than the circumstances themselves. For executives in the decision-making seat, rarely do your choices for action or behavior impact only you—there is an unavoidable ripple effect to others. The higher you are on the ladder, the broader and deeper the impact—good or bad—you will have. What we think drives what we do—and who we are—as we do it. When we interact with others understand this: We teach people how to treat us and think of us. If you're a leader, this will determine whether people follow you and do their best for you—or not.

Early in my career, I was the top producer in the country for a leading mortgage banking company. While I enjoyed a great relationship with my manager and co-workers, I had a problem: My approach that I used when working through a difference of opinion with the team that processed my brokers' loans was seen as combative. It seemed that while I was quite adept at making my case in a forceful, airtight manner worthy of the great defense attorney Clarence Darrow, I was also masterful at igniting a threat response in the mind of the person who had to engage with me. Thus, many in the team dreaded having to call me when a loan was headed for denial and they knew, more than likely, I would challenge them on that decision. It didn't matter that 99 percent of the time I was right. It wasn't about being right. The important point here was the way in which I went about making my case was provoking avoidance behavior in my team. I am not proud that I ever behaved this way but there you have it—not my finest hour.

Fortunately, I quickly evolved away from that behavior because by my side was the best manager of my career, Neil Coleman. He challenged me to figure out how to see things differently and made me realize that I could be right in what my point was and wrong in the way I was expressing it. He had a way of raising your awareness that left your self-esteem intact and your mind challenged to think in a better direction. How I invited people to see things differently was a choice. So I asked myself some questions: "What hand do I have in what I am experiencing with my team?" "How am I thinking about them that is getting in the way?" and then, "What can I do to shift the way I engage them that doesn't provoke fear and avoidance?" I shifted my approach from trying to be right to being curious about how the other person saw the situation and hopefully igniting their curiosity to understand my perspective as well. In the end, they felt heard and valued. They felt I trusted and respected their opinion. After that mind shift, I became the person the teams wanted to work with and many sought to get assigned to my region so they could do so.

By building awareness and connection between one's thinking/feeling processes and then developing agility in the way we activate that connection when working with others, we will become more adept at achieving important change and moving people to do their best. Building mental agility begins with the questions we ask ourselves before, during and after we come face-to-face with our challenges.

What I hope you embrace by the end of this book is this:

1. We are not stuck with all the stories we tell ourselves that drive the thinking that produces results that are not no longer working for us and others – and perhaps never did. We don't have to cling to beliefs that are chiseling out a smaller and narrower line of sight that blinds us to better options for better results.

2. The thinking we use that works in one situation (or worked in the past) may not now.

3. We do have this gift, our brain, which is primed and ready to develop the power to adapt and flow with change, uncertainty, adversity and ambiguity.

I'm hoping what you read in these pages, even if it's just one chapter that resonates with you, catalyzes you to action to begin to shift your mental gears. Starting with powerful questions you can choose to access the richer thinking that resides within you right now. If you choose to challenge yourself to develop agility in the way you think about what is—and see a path to what it can be—I promise you will be better for it.

There is a quote by Martin Luther King, Jr. that I love: "In the end, we will not remember the words of our enemies, but the silence of our friends." I believe this also relates to our thinking. We cannot silence our best self with thinking that makes us be less and create less by holding us hostage with beliefs that we are afraid to challenge with powerful questions and live into with courageous action.

Our best is yet to come. I want to contribute to activating that potential within us.

SECTION
ONE

Why Take the Journey?

Success or failure is not about the circumstances. It's more often about how you choose to think about them that determines how well things turn out.

CHAPTER 1

Tommy's Story: An Airman's Mind Shift Saga

The squadron of eleven B-29 bombers took to the air at 0330 on December 14, 1944 and soon approached its targets over Japanese-held Burma. This was supposed to be a "milk run"—a routine mission. That assessment couldn't have been more off target.

It was Tommy's turn to move to the bomb bay hatch door of his plane, Gambler's Choice, and peer through the small glass window. His task was to ensure the bombs were away and to let the bombardier know that no bombs were still hung up in the bay. He looked through the small window as the orders "Bombs away!" were given. In one moment, all the bombs dropped away from the bay, the swinging bay gates waving good-bye as the high-explosives plummeted toward their targets. Tommy turned to make the call to the bombardier and suddenly—a deafening explosion.

Tommy was immediately pinned to the floor as the hulking B-29 flipped in the air. The sky was red with flames from burning fuel, his hand was bloody, and air was rushing all around. Tommy made his way to the swinging bomb bay hatch door and looked down through the open bomb gates. The bomber was in a flat spin spiraling toward earth. He saw bodies some with parachutes, some horridly not, hurtling past the open gates as he realized that he had to act—now. He had to parachute to save his life using the empty bomb bay as his escape route.

He turned toward the other crew and to his best friend, Vernon, yelling, "Are you coming?"

Vernon answered, "Yes, go, go! I'm right behind you!"

Centrifugal force pushed Tommy back into the plane but Tommy fiercely grabbed hold of the sides of the bomb bay opening and with all his strength pulled himself downward out of the plane. He shot into the air, tumbling and keeping watch as the spiraling plane came around again toward him. Finally he saw it was clear and pulling the ripcord, activated the chute. But in his confusion and haste to get out of the plane, he made a major error: He had forgotten to refasten his chest strap to secure his upper body when the chute deployed. Upon activation, the chute yanked Tommy upward and, because his chest strap was unfastened, he fell out of the arm harness and hung upside down. He was descending rapidly only hanging by his legs but finally got himself upright by grabbing his pants leg and working his way back upright. He got a hold of his straps and just hung on trying to regain his senses. Tommy was light-headed as the oxygen was thin at that altitude. He got lost in the momentary silence and the realization that he saw no more chutes coming out of his plane. He watched in horror whispering, "Please, please let me see someone else getting out of that plane." But there were none. With great sadness, he saw Gambler's Choice spin in a fiery, smoking descent into a final explosion. The realization crashed through the silence of the air around him. He knew that he lost some of his closest friends, Vern being the best of them. As he looked out across the Burmese jungle that was coming closer into view, Tommy's thoughts drifted to what brought him to this moment.

"Please, please let me see someone else getting out of that plane." But there were none.

Tommy was born in Manhattan in 1924. He was the only child of immigrant parents of Armenian descent. Because no one could remember his Armenian name, Karnig, he was often called "Tommy" due to his last name being Thomasian. His father owned his own business in the city. He created fine beaded and sequined designs which were carefully sewn onto gowns in the top fashion houses

Tommy in uniform, age 18.

in New York City. His mother was a piano teacher and a woman with an intuitive mind that was way ahead of her time. Both parents had a great influence on Tommy. His father— one of Theodore Roosevelt's Rough Riders—had a quiet dignity and honest work ethic that was respected in his professional circles. His mother had a kind heart and a sharp wit spiked with practical jokes. She was also a forward-thinking person who asked Tommy questions about his life and shared her views. She encouraged him to think about his own choices and behaviors. She challenged him when he did wrong and listened when he needed compassion. Both parents gave him a healthy respect of all people, which was supported by the very diverse neighborhood of immigrants who had also come to this country seeking a new life.

When Tommy was eighteen, he had a job working in a factory as a riveter working the night shift building Catalina bombers. He felt this was his way of doing his part in aiding the war effort. One day, the union boss saw that he wasn't taking his smoking break like the others. The foreman barked at him, asking him why he wasn't on break to which Tommy responded, "I don't smoke."

At this remark, the foreman became upset and threatened to not approve him to join the union unless he put his tools down and took a break. Tommy looked him square in the eye and asked, "Don't you care that a war is going on? They need what we're building so what's wrong if I am willing to keep working?"

The foreman glared at him repeating his threat about the union. Confused, Tommy took his break and contemplated what had happened. He just couldn't be with people like this and still look at himself in the mirror. So a week later on November 6, 1942 he quit the job, left high school, and volunteered to join the Army Air Corps. He discussed his decision with his parents and, realizing his deep commitment, they gave their blessings as long as he promised to finish his last term of high school after his military service. How excited he was! He decided to pursue a flight engineer route. Even though he'd be up against guys who went to college and he hadn't yet finished high school, he really wanted to go for it so he hunkered down and studied hard. Tommy had a higher purpose that fueled his will to give this a shot. He believed that this was how he was going to become a good man. Serving others and making sure that the planes were sound

B-29 Bomber

Image is from Airforce Image Gallery and have been modified and can be found at Planes of World War II page

for our pilots flying to defend our country and bring them home safe to their families. This was his thinking that drove his choices to join the war effort. Three weeks after he finished his initial training in Chanute Field, IL he was shipped out to Seattle to the Boeing plant and it is there that he learned of The Flying Superfortress—the B-29 bomber that was just beginning to roll off the factory lines and was being tested. Though he failed some of the technical exams, he did pass the ones he needed to in order to become an Electrical Specialist/Gunner on the B-29. He was eventually assigned to his own B-29 named Gambler's Choice. Two years later on December 13, 1944, Tommy's squadron received orders to fly a mission to drop bombs on Rangoon, Burma. They were to leave on December 14, 1944.

Tommy's mind was snapped back to the present by his sudden awareness of bullets whizzing by his head and body as he continued to plummet toward the area where Japanese soldiers were gathered. With a jolt, he realized the Japanese were shooting at the men as they descended out of the sky. Tommy looked up and saw that there was a v-cut in the strap right above him. A bullet had pierced it just a few inches from his head. He decided to become less of a target and curled his body into a ball eyeing the field where he was likely to land. On the way down, he thought of a plan to get to a station on the north coast that had provisions for this kind of emergency. Tommy hit the ground in a field of rice paddies. He shed his parachute and began to run for the coast but was quickly surrounded by an army of local peasants who took him and presented him to the Japanese soldiers. They tied his hands behind his back. At the precise point that his freedom was taken from him was when he truly understood the value of such a gift.

Upon arriving at Rangoon Central Jail, he and others were stripped, searched, interrogated, beaten, and put into solitary. He eventually was put into a cell with one of his crew who survived, Norm. Of course, starvation, further interrogations, and beatings ensued but Tommy kept thinking of ways to survive, to prepare for what might come next. Fear was his enemy and eventually, his enemy began to gain some ground in his mind. Did anyone know what happened and where we were? Were they coming to get us? What was going to happen to us? These and other uncertainties racked his mind, and the minds of all the POWs.

Days dragged on to months as Tommy, standing at six feet, withered to 120 pounds. He wasted away just like everyone else who was imprisoned there. Those imprisoned, the Chinese, British RAF, and Americans, began to wonder how many more suns would rise over their captivity. For some, their thoughts began turning to desperation, futility, and hopelessness. Then, there came the pivotal moment that re-awakened Tommy's thinking and became the lightning rod for a critical shift in his attitude and actions. Tommy noticed that there were some men who were brought into the compound broken, with the blood dripping through the makeshift stretchers made of leaves and branches from the jungle that somehow survived with little-to-no medical care. Yet, other prisoners with no noticeable wounds would go into their cell, lie down, face the wall, and be dead in two days. It came to Tommy in a flash of insight: These men gave up mentally. They told themselves the story of "I can't" and "no hope." They couldn't imagine a future beyond their present circumstances and so they became a true prisoner, held hostage by the daily beatings, starvation, uncertainty and mental anguish.

Tommy made a decision in that moment to tell himself a different story, which became his vision and purpose: *"This is not where I'm going to die. I am going home and I will see my family again and I'm going to help as many guys as I can go with me."* And with that, he shifted his thinking to create a new habit of mind that drove him to make better choices each day. Once he engaged this new way of seeing his circumstances, he realized that he had control of what he thought about them. He began to ask different questions,

"He began to ask different questions, which helped him make better decisions...taking actions that he could control that would help him endure his current reality."

which helped him make better decisions as to how he would move about each day engaging in behaviors and taking actions that he could control that would help him endure his current reality and increase his chances of achieving his vision: Going home and embracing his family again. He chose to believe. He chose to think differently about what he had to face daily.

Throughout his time in prison camp, Tommy and others were put in the execution stance on their knees many times. Each time, he thought his end was only a few breaths away as he felt the cold steel of a sword resting on his neck. Another time, a Japanese prison guard cornered Tommy in his cell and shoved the business end of a rifle at the base of his skull; laughing, the guard said he was going to kill him now and then pulled the trigger on an empty chamber. Tommy passed out right then. But Tommy had made the decision that he was going to make it home and he kept his mind on his goal: "I'm going home. I'm going to see my family again and I'm going to help as many guys as I can do the same." Did he have fear and nightmares? Of course he did. Did he struggle with keeping his goal crystal clear and getting through each horrific day? Yes, at times he did. But he kept the mantra going. He kept the picture in his mind that would help him endure what he saw and what he felt physically, emotionally, and mentally.

The rest is history. With the growing impact the American B-29s were having in the power of their bombing payload and the advancing British armies making their way south from Mandalay, the Japanese realized the end was near. In 1945, the Japanese evacuated the Rangoon prison camp, taking with them those that could walk and leaving behind the weaker and barely surviving prisoners. Tommy was one of them. When he and another fellow prisoner realized that their captors had gone, they scoped out the compound before letting the other prisoners know. Though he was suffering from swollen legs and feet due to gangrene, Tommy and his friend carefully inspected the camp to ensure there were no remaining Japanese or booby traps. Upon doing so, they heard planes coming in overhead and realized they were allied planes. "Hallelujah! They're coming for us!"

Then cheers turned to horror as bombs began to drop.

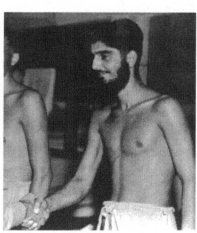
Tommy after his liberation

The allies didn't realize that the only people in this camp were allied prisoners. Quickly Tommy and a buddy found the supply hut, got white paint, and scrambled up onto the roofs of two prison houses and painted the following phrases: *Japs Gone. Extract Digit.* At that point, the bombing stopped and food and medical supplies were parachute-dropped into the camp.

Soon, they were liberated. Tommy is seen above a few days after his liberation at a hospital in Calcutta. In the end, he and other men who endured their time as POWs finally came home. Tommy fulfilled his vision of hugging his family and knew that other men were doing the same.

Life-altering experiences leave their mark on us. What we do with it is the opportunity we all have. Will we be victimized by our painful experiences and live a less vibrant and powerful life under a cloud of fear, anger and doubt? Or will we forge a foundation of strength from which we will build a way of thinking that will create the best possible life and contributions that we can? Not many of us will face the kind of extreme circumstance that Tommy did; however, everything is relative, right? We all will face some challenge that we each will consider extreme for us. Let's look at how developing an agile mindset gives you the best shot at becoming the victor, not the victim, regardless of circumstances you are facing now and will throughout your life.

In the last chapter I will return to conclude Tommy's story to tell you what he made of this experience and how it shaped his life.

CHAPTER 2

Why Do You Need an Agile Mind?

The necessity for leaders to make the right decisions in the midst of the ambiguity and uncertainty of our world has never been more in demand. With the volatility and complexity of emerging domestic and global developments and innovations, the challenge of making the right decisions starts to become even more intense. As a leader, how do you develop the ability to, on the one hand, stay true to your values and at the same time, adapt and flow with the shape-shifting environment to meet the demands of a world in flux? How do you do all that and still live a life that is authentic to you?

Time was when something was tried and true and if it worked once it would work again. Command and control leadership, for example, was the typical way leaders drove their companies to success. Is that approach alone still relevant to our current marketplace and emerging workforce dynamics? I think there are certain things that shouldn't change, like values that endure across time, geography, culture, and circumstance. Values such as honor, integrity, honesty, ethics, courage, and authenticity never go out of style, if we can refer to those precious aspects of human character in fashion terms. For leadership and management practices, though, being stuck in one gear doesn't suffice anymore. Even business models and internal processes have to be revisited more often due to the velocity of change that is accelerated by unprecedented innovations in technology and global connectedness. We expect action and responses quicker in the midst of more complexity and ambiguity while still expecting decision-makers to figure out and choose the right path.

For leaders, it is increasingly critical for them to develop the neural prowess and agility for dealing with the twists and turns of the ever changing business highway—taking what they have known to be true, plucking out what is still relevant, and then letting the rest of their thinking be open for reworking. This requires one foundational shift that must happen before all else: Decision-makers and influencers must see the prospect of challenging their thinking and deeply held beliefs in a new light— something that will make them stronger not weaker. Presently and looking forward, we need to see ambiguity as an opportunity to shape clarity instead of being seen as a blurry mess that clouds vision and thinking. To see uncertainty as a portal for asking provocative questions that challenge our thinking by asking, "Will the way I've done this before work now?" To see volatility as the spark that ignites the mind out of its complacency.

One of my clients is coming face-to-face with this question. They have seen significant growth over the last decade. They are an organization of dedicated, passionate, brilliant people who work in an industry that is experiencing tectonic shifts and uncertainty. A frequent topic of discussion I have with the executives of this organization revolves around raising their awareness around the stories and mindsets that got them where they are – both good and now, some challenging. They are poised to accelerate their growth because of the great work they've done in delivering on their promise to their clients year after year. Now they are beginning to experience the tension and initial cracks that come from the new realities of being successful—more work volume, diminishing capacity in their staff and underpinning processes that are not properly supporting their current and growing needs. They are at a pivotal point. Which way it will go will largely rest on the shoulders of the decision-makers to deeply challenge their thinking, take risks, and trust each other while maintaining their core values, quality of delivery, and identity.

An agile and adaptable way of seeing the world and our place in it is critical not only for our survival but mostly to give us the power to amp our ability to thrive. As a leader, you must lubricate your brain with mental challenges that will grow your mindset and make it more agile. Building a more nimble mind will enable you to more fluidly access valuable input from what the various regions of your brain have in store for you. When you think about it, as a human race, we wouldn't have made it this far without being able to adapt to a changing environment, creating innovations that came from accidental trial and error—crude as they may have been in the beginning. This means you have an inherent ability to adapt, learn, create, and innovate if you just connect with those resources. To see change as an opportunity to raise you up instead of a threat to bring you down. The more you tap into your immense ability to adapt and flow with change, the more mentally agile and fit you will become to keep pace with the demands of a world that is in constant flux. Anywhere, anytime, with anyone.

> *An agile and adaptable way of seeing the world and our place in it is critical not only for our survival but mostly to give us the power to amp our ability to thrive.*

As it turns out to be, our brains can always build new wiring, no matter your age. And that new wiring can take hold and bypass old neural highways we've developed. A saying in neuroscience states that "neurons that fire together, wire together." Once we wire our "story" about certain situations or people or events or even ourselves, it becomes "brain sticky." The more we repeat that story, the stickier and more hard-wired it gets and the more it becomes the lens through which we look at the world. Stories become the filter for incoming experiences and help us make meaning of them so we can decide how we will feel about them and take action. *(While I'm talking brain here, let me share an important scientific fact which many executives will find inconvenient, scoff-worthy and shocking. Based on many studies and research, 90 percent of our decisions are made by our emotional brain. That is not a typo— that really is ninety. We utilize our rational brain to think up logical reasons why what we feel has merit.)* But what if those stories aren't working for you anymore? What if those stories are actually sabotaging your success? They perhaps worked for you at some point and then ever so slowly, little by little, the outcomes that they used to produce start to be harder to come by. They don't work as well and, one day, backfire on you and others. You sit there asking yourself: "How did this happen? Why didn't this work? Why is this so hard now?" It's like a very slow leak in your tire. You're driving along fine and then all of a sudden, *pow!* You're riding on your rim and it's not pretty. If you blow out in the middle of the highway at

5 p.m. rush hour on a hot day, causing a fender bender and a two-mile back-up, you are going to be the recipient of hand gestures and epithets in many languages because, you know, we live in a very diverse world now. If you're lucky, you will be in a lane where you can pull over and assess the damage. Hopefully you have a spare, AAA roadside assistance, or a really good friend to whom you'll end up owing a beer.

It happens the same way when you are a leader. If you haven't ever challenged the way you've been thinking, especially if you're a first time C-suite executive, you run the risk of blowing out in the middle of business traffic where your downfall will be quite visible potentially causing a ripple effect to the organization (and your career) that could be damaging and expensive. Marshall Goldsmith wrote a book called, *What Got You Here Won't Get You There*. All you need to read is that title and you get it, don't you? When you climb the ladder (and as you get older) there are things that will be asked of you and expected of you that haven't been asked before. You're going to need to evolve by advancing your mindset, behaviors and emotional regulation.

One of the most important truths about being an executive leader today is that you have to be ready for anything. The ugly truth in the executive suite, which I have been privy to as an executive coach, is this: Those who step into the shoes of an executive role feel an enormous vulnerability to their status, one of the brain's threat/reward dimensions that will be discussed later, as well as a huge responsibility to always be right and have the answers. The stakes are high and a lot is riding on their ability to make the right call. They are scared to let people down—their family, their team, the person who hired them. They don't want to lose what their position enables them to be, do and have. And so, many executives tell themselves: "Don't mess this up." This is a very isolating story and a very limiting one, especially when projects, initiatives, and careers start to show the first signs of the wheels coming off. The truth is: being an effective executive does not mean you have to come up with all the answers; you do have to be wise and adept enough to know how to find them and deliver them. It means you will figure out how to course-correct when you inevitably go off-track. This means, you will not figure it all out alone. You will need others.

Here's where the rewiring for mental agility has to come in, especially when markets are in motion, leadership changes, competition ramps up and when you find yourself in circumstances that you did not create. This is where the power of the questions you ask yourself comes into play. You will find that in life, the only thing you control is how you make meaning and deal with what is in front of you, whether you created it or not. Making the best of what is by finding your way to your best thinking can be the difference between success or failure; landing the job or being an also-ran; keeping a friend or losing one; building a strong reputation or destroying it. What helps set our course is to be clear about our big picture and purpose. To develop habits of mind that ignite our creative spark and which give us the power to not only survive but thrive. That higher goal serves as the true north to guide the choices we make in the present with an eye to our desired future. Clarity of purpose and vision give us the fuel to endure what we must.

Anyone can do this. But not everyone will. I'm not going to kid you—despite all efforts and best thinking and intentions, sometimes things don't work out as planned and for the moment we are left wincing from the pain and the fallout. Still there is something to learn, isn't there, if you have the will to look? You can deal with and make the best of challenges and opportunities. Let's not forget how often people are handed a great opportunity and still blow it. So you need to approach even good opportunities with an agile mind as well. To have your best shot at coming out on top despite the circumstances, you need three things: The will to become aware of your current thought patterns, the discipline to challenge yourself with powerful questions to develop your mental agility, and the courage to apply what your learn to the situation at hand.

To give you confidence that you can develop agile thinking, the next sections will speak to our brain's incredible ability to change, rewire and grow new connections.

A FEW KEY POINTS ABOUT THE HUMAN BRAIN

For purposes of providing context and connecting points to what I will share with you throughout this book, here are some basic insights into that magnificent brain that sits between your ears. Understanding some basics about the brain will help you appreciate your own potential and understand why you respond the way you do to what is going on around you. Even this elementary grasp of how the brain works will help give you confidence to challenge your existing beliefs and be able to catch yourself when sabotaging thoughts start creeping in to derail you. You can begin to redirect your thinking with powerful questions that I will pose in later chapters that will tap into the wisdom you have right now.

Let's Use Our Whole Brain

How do you develop an agile mind? How do you release the brakes on your current thinking and speed up the process of building new neural wiring that will help you navigate the road ahead? Here's a basic life fact: You don't always control *what* happens out there. You do, however, control the *meaning you make* of what happens out there and what you ultimately do about it. Developing a nimble mindset will improve your ability to adjust and recalibrate your perspective and thinking, regulate your emotions to help you make the best decisions possible along the way—or at the very least cope as positively as possible until you figure it out. As Dan Pink said in his book, *A Whole New Mind*, the right brain is rising and joining its left-side counterpart in the spotlight. Our right brain is getting the respect it deserves now that newer technology allows us to really understand how the our brain functions as a highly integrated unit and the value we can bring when we truly engage what our whole brain has to offer.

Let's take a quick tour of this magnificent gift called the human brain so you get some basic information about your most valuable resource that you can access at any time, every day and even works for you when you sleep.

The left brain, it is generally accepted, is all about logic and reasoning, one premise leading to the next. (Picture cubicles with people in it who are studying facts and figures.) It is sequential with a focus on data and detail. It enables us to compartmentalize data into neat pockets of information that "go together." It is like a serial processor. The right brain by contrast is the seat of our emotions and social self. It looks at the big picture and makes inferences. It "plays" with information that is incoming and that which has been stored. (Picture colorful open fields with people playing, dancing, freely exploring.) The right brain also connects seemingly disconnected pieces of information and puts them together into a picture. It is like a parallel processor. It perceives patterns among data. It has a "knowing" that often is faster than the logical brain.

Unfortunately, we are not taught to trust our creative brain and emotional circuitry as much as our left, rational brain. This is to our detriment. Our emotions give us data—very important data that we need in order to make the best decisions. Why? Our emotional brain has an intellect uniquely wired to certain parts of our brain to tell us how we feel about what is going on and what judgments we have made. As was mentioned in a previous chapter, some brain researchers have postulated that 90 percent of our decision-making is emotion-based. We use our rational brain to come up with logical rationalizations as to why we make a decision that was driven by our emotions. You probably aren't aware of this, but this is how it goes. We are persuaded by logic; we are moved by emotion. Believe me when I tell you that I have witnessed very logical people become quite emotional about people who aren't being logical.

Think of your neurons (86 billion of them) as UPS drivers: They are trying to deliver something to you. Based on your experiences, these drivers are dispatched to deliver their package. That package, at times, is holding a message called your emotional thinking. It may be some right brain parallel-processed thinking that doesn't seem to have all the data to back it up and yet, there's that *feeling* that you know you need to pay attention to it. So, you need to answer the door, take the package, and open it up. You may send it back after you inspect the message, try it on, or work with it; or you may end up keeping all or part of it. You see, it's not an either/or thing when talking about various regions of our brain—we need our whole brain to function optimally. That is because "all right brain" and "all left brain" thinking just isn't enough, especially these days with the complexity and speed of our lives and the demands that are continually raising the stakes.

The best part is, you can open yourself to the power of what your whole brain gives you and there is a component that is built into your brain that will facilitate that as it does every day whether you know it or not: the Corpus Callosum. Think of the Corpus Callosum as a bridge across which neural activity from the left and right brain meet, mingle, and communicate to make even more connections there. The brain is constantly sending data and signals back and forth through this neural hotspot. Here's the best news: You can amp up that communication very simply by getting into a meditative state. You may not think so, but you do this all the time. Have you ever been in the shower and all of a sudden ideas come to you? Or you suddenly figure out a solution to a problem when you're exercising or the answer to a question pops up suddenly while you're fixing your car? That's because you are suspending all the left brain work of "thinking about it" so hard and you are freeing up your whole brain to plumb the depths of your subconscious and other regions of your brain. The gates open and it's like Happy Hour at the corpus callosum—lots of mixing and mingling. When you go to sleep with a problem or question on your mind, many times the first thing you think of in the morning is the answer to the question or the thing you were trying to remember the night before.

What I hope for you to take away from this chapter, and this book, is a new respect for your whole brain and all that you may be leaving untapped that is there for you. Waiting. The three pound gift that rests on your neck has the power to take you where you want to go by developing the inherent agility it has to move between different ways of thinking and seeing what you encounter. It can open doors to your best self, your best thinking. It can help you heal, help you redefine the traumas of your past, as well as harness your successes— forging them both into a rock solid foundation upon which you can choose to build the life you want to live. As a leader you can access this ability to build a vital career and make the impact you want to have. All you need is one thing to activate it: The will to go there. You must be willing to challenge your beliefs, your thinking, your stories, and what you have been holding onto as "fact." You must be willing to accept that in order to find your way to right, sometimes, you must be willing to risk being wrong.

Our Brain's Organizing Principle: Threat versus Reward

Neuroscience, as discussed in David Rock's 2008 book, *Your Brain at Work*, is exploding with new revelations about our brain, scientifically showing that what we think directly influences what we do. For executive decision-makers, this is critical learning. Our patterns of thinking (which combine emotional responses as well as logical analysis) inform our decisions and drive our choices and actions. How we repeatedly respond to certain people, for example, is due to how we repeatedly think of them, which may be based on previous experience with that person. We already begin an internal dialogue about them, sometimes before they've even opened their mouths. Our brains have set the stage for what is about to transpire. This is why it's hard for people who have made a bad impression over time (and it doesn't take much time) to ever get out of the "box" our brains put them in. (Not to mention the box we put ourselves in.) We become hardwired with our thinking toward that person. It's the same for how we think about theories, problems, relationships, challenges, politics, etc. And there's a reason for this: Bad is stronger than good (as it turns out about three to five times stronger). Our brain's organizing principle is to run away from threat and walk toward reward. Threat can kill you; reward can just make you feel good. It is also important to know that the brain processes many social threats and rewards with the same intensity as physical threats and rewards, as Matthew D. Lieberman and Naomi I. Eisenberger discussed in their 2009 *Science* article, "Pains and Pleasures of Social Life." In other words, humiliating a person in front of others is as painful to their brain as slapping them across the face. This goes for you too.

David Rock created the SCARF model, which talks about five dimensions across which our brain's experience threat (avoid) or reward (approach) responses:

- **Status** (our standing relative to others)
- **Certainty** (our sense of being able to predict what is going to happen next)
- **Autonomy** (our sense of control, having a say or choice about what happens to us or others we care about)
- **Relatedness** (a sense of friend not foe, trust, being from similar tribe)
- **Fairness** (a sense of equitable exchange between humans)

It is this neural dynamic that informs our thinking and triggers emotions and physical responses which we use to make sense out of what is being presented to us every day. Our responses to what gets stimulated along this continuum of threat/reward is also what shapes our decisions inside our heads and moves us to make specific choices, engage in certain behaviors, and then take certain actions externally, which are observable and felt by others.

To give you a quick illustration of how the dimensions get triggered and what some of the internal dialog might sound like in a threat state, here is an example: You are a senior executive who has to announce a big change that will encompass the likelihood that certain jobs will be outsourced. You would do well to consider the following:

There is an inherent big hit to Certainty. People's minds will begin to swirl around questions like: What will happen to me? How will I provide for my family given the horrible employment market? I hate interviewing! Who will be my boss? Will I make the cut? There is also a potential hit to Status and Autonomy: Will they consolidate the management? Will I be demoted and lose my standing and title I worked so hard to achieve? I like the direct access I have to my boss and the say I have in some of the decisions we make as a leadership team. We didn't get a chance to offer our ideas for a better solution. Great, I might even lose my budget and the ability to guide what happens in my department. Relatedness and Fairness also are ignited driving these thoughts: Makes me feel good that I am part of the "in-group". Now I'm going to lose that. I really thought this guy would have our backs. I guess you really can't trust anyone. Really? After all we have done to just decide to send our jobs overseas? Totally unfair.

These are just the threats to those *receiving* the message. As the one who must make the announcement, you need to go through each dimension and ask yourself what is getting triggered for you in *delivering* this message? Once you understand which threats are impacting your thinking, the next step is to focus on how you could talk about this announcement in a way that dials down the fear they (and you) are feeling and redirect their minds to a more positive (reward) frame of mind. You won't be able to always reduce certain feelings of threat however, you can lessen the blow and give everyone (and yourself) a different way to see it and be with it to help you all move forward more productively.

So this begs the question: Can we change our hardwiring around this threat/reward way of being with the world? Right now science says mostly, no. But the good news is our brains can build new wiring around how we *deal* with it. And it doesn't take as long as we previously thought to construct new neural highways over which our thoughts can travel. The more we use these new roadways and continue to build upon them, the more hardwired they become. What happens, then, is that we are more quickly able to access these roads of thought to move our decisions, choices, and actions in a direction that will create for us (and perhaps our business, results, team, family, or society) new and better outcomes.

NOW HEAR THIS—YOUR BRAIN IS BUILT FOR CHANGE AND GROWTH

Carol Dweck, in her 2014 book *Mindset*, discusses the importance of growth versus fixed mindsets. It is important to know that despite our hesitancy and blind spots around change and our need to do so, our brains are designed to build new wiring to enable change to happen. There is so much neural robustness waiting for us to engage that it is almost unimaginable. Think about all that wiring and the synapses I talked about earlier. It's all there—for you—now. You don't need more budget, resources, territory, better pricing, or better staff. You don't need to be smarter, taller, richer, better-looking, stronger, and have a better title—you just need the will to develop better thinking about whatever it is you're facing.

Dweck reveals in the outcomes of decades of research that a fixed mindset is in control when executives walk around with a tape in their head that says: "Whatever you do, look smart and talented at all cost—don't do anything dumb." This sets the stage for staying within a zone of thinking that is quite narrow. Worse, it is what this person will expect from others and the climate they will create within the existing culture. A growth mindset on the other hand sounds more like this: Learn at all cost. We need to see failure as a friend from whom we learn who helps us get to the right answer faster. A fixed mindset worries more about self-preservation in the face of perceived fear than self-evolution and improvement. People with a fixed mindset are more concerned about being the best. Growth mindset people, as Dweck states, are about getting better; a continual march toward improvement, which includes episodes of learning from mistakes and setbacks. And what of those setbacks? Fixed mindset people see them as something to hide. They internalize a setback as saying something bad about them. Those with a growth mindset see setbacks as something to learn from; a gift that is a natural part of learning along the way to success.

Anyone can choose to develop a growth mindset in themselves or others. Again, you just need the will to do so and the courage to apply what you develop to the challenges you're facing.

SECTION
TWO

The Road Trip to Building Agility

Here begins our road trip. The following chapters will seek to prime your mental gears with questions, stories, and challenges so that you can make the best of what you encounter along the way. This kind of mental exercise— seeing your situation in different ways—will begin to develop your mental agility. Developing your mental agility will, in turn, make your mind more nimble, giving you increased likelihood of figuring out the best path in a volatile, complex, uncertain and ambiguous world.

CHAPTER 3

Getting Ready to Take the Trip

WARMING UP THE ENGINE

I believe where we will find our power to do our best thinking that drives our best decision-making is not so much in the answers we end up with but in the questions we ask ourselves to begin with. In the coming chapters, you will discover stories of some great "Mind Shifters," some of whom are my clients. Additionally, you will find some methodologies that will begin to prime your mental gears to become more adept at processing possibilities, realities, and uncertainty as well as heighten your awareness of your own thinking in the moment. At the end of each chapter will be a section called Mind *Shift*. This will be a set of questions, suggestions, or a request that will help you challenge your current thinking and open up the neural gateways to other possibilities and potential. Let's get ready to hit the road.

What you will need:

- Commitment to open your mind to what you will read.

- A way to capture your thoughts and insights as you move through this book such as a journaling book, recording device, or an app on your smart phone.

- Surroundings in which you can think and focus without disruption.

- A five-minute practice you already have in place for meditating or calming your mind and body or a recording of a five-minute (or more if you need it) meditation you can listen to. Have it cued up ready to go in the future when you want to do this work.

I'd like you to first prepare your mind to be open. This will only take five minutes. If you have a favorite five minute meditation that you do or a way of clearing your mind that works for you. Please do your meditation now. Allow other thoughts to just fade away or sit to the side.

Done? Let's begin.

PICK A LANE

I know that everyone has a lot of mental traffic that is made of demands and desires that jockey for position as the most important priority you have to pay attention to. For purposes of our work together here, I'd like you to think of just one situation, professionally or personally, that you have been dealing with and for which you have yet to create a satisfying outcome. Or you may know the outcome you wish to achieve but the first steps seem unclear or too hard to take. It can be a challenge at work, at home, or with a friend. It could be in your volunteer work or just within yourself. It could be a task, project, or a personal relationship.

Make a note of it now.

As you move through this book, use this situation as the context for your thinking when you get to the Mind *Shift* sections in each chapter.

Going forward, you are going to be reading about ways to increase your brain's agility but I am not leaving it at that. I am going to challenge you to put it into action to create that mental muscle memory. Going through "what if" scenarios, not just mentally but also physically, can preload the brain with circuitry to call on should the unexpected arise. This is why diving instructors take their students on a dive and while underwater rip off their masks so that they learn not to panic and engage the proper counter measures to handle the situation successfully. Engaging the brain by actually going through it, increases the likelihood that the practice beforehand has wired enough for you to call on it to be there for you. That's the reason for the Mind *Shift* sections at the end of each chapter. It's my way of compelling you to develop ways to create agility in the way you are thinking and then taking what this new mental approach gives you for a test drive by applying it

Going through "what if" scenarios, not just mentally but also physically, can preload the brain with circuitry to call on should the unexpected arise.

as often as possible to experience it. Not just once, but over and over. Practice doesn't make perfect. Practice makes new neural wiring that will serve you. By practicing, you reinforce that new wiring more and more every time you engage your mind and your actions in these exercises.

KNOW YOUR DESTINATION— THE BIG PICTURE

Before starting out on any big trip, it's good to know where you want to end up. What do you want to get out of the experience? What do you want the outcome to be? One of the first steps of building an agile mind is clarifying what the purpose is of doing so. What is your vision that will guide you along the way? Who are you trying to become? What do you expect to shift as a result of bringing agility and adaptability to the way you think about what comes across your path in business and in life? Leaders need to think about this. As you rise up the corporate ladder, your experiences will change and leave their mark on your mind. What is required of you becomes more dimensional and tricky and goes beyond seeing possibilities solely in terms of either/or solution paths. The world becomes more complex, more variables enter into your picture, and ambiguity soars. The stakes are higher, the expectations more intense, and the world just keeps shape-shifting, making static thinking obsolete on any day without warning. It's easy to feel off-balance, swerving from one lane to another and unable to see the next turn clearly. Or perhaps you are stuck in neutral unable to pop the clutch on any decision for action. So it's important to start with your *Why* and the big picture which will serve as the litmus tests to apply to ideas and options when you have to deal with unexpected situations that require a decision. You can ask yourself: Does this option lead me toward my desired outcome? Yes/no. If no, dump the option. If yes, how? Is that a viable option? Are there others that could get me there too? If you don't have a clear picture of what your desired outcome looks like specifically, how are you going to evaluate options that come before you let alone think them up?

Many times, clients come to me and spend a good deal of time explaining the time they have spent spinning their wheels trying to decide among options they have identified for a particular situation. So, I ask them questions— remember the power is in the question—and I'm going to ask them of you now.

MIND *SHIFT*

Think about the situation I asked you to bring to this work.

QUESTION ONE: On a scale of one to ten, with ten being crystal clear, how clear are you about the outcome you want to achieve in the situation you selected to focus on?

Make note of it now.

QUESTION TWO: Regarding your chosen situation, define your ten (desired outcome). Break it down into categories. Categories could be anything. Think of all the components of your situation that need to come together to create your "ten." For example, if you are focusing on getting an initiative to completion your categories might be: the team members you select, your role and what you have to remember as a leader, budget, other outcomes, etc. For now, just list all the categories and describe what "ten" looks like for each one in detail. Spend some time thinking about this. Don't rush if you can help it. If your number in question one is below seven, you need more clarity on what your desired outcome is. After all, how will you know what you need for the trip if you're not clear about where you're going and what that destination looks like?

YOU ARE HERE

I'm sure many of you have had this experience. You're at a mall and you know your destination is a particular store. You look at that big directory (which is curiously never where you need it to be) and you've identified where the store is in the gigantic mall. Now, how to best get there? Your brain wants to know, "Where am I in relation to that store?" You look for those words: *You Are Here.* You see it and sometimes, you even put your finger on the icon. Suddenly, you can map out how to get from where you are to where you want to be. Things fall into place and decisions as to which way to go become very clear, very quickly. Well, it's like that in the situation you're facing here. You've got your desired destination clearly in mind now, what it looks like, what it will be like, and what is needed. Now you need to get there from here but where is here for you? You need to put your finger on it.

MIND *SHIFT*

Now on a scale of one to ten, where ten is the desired outcome you described above, rate where you are now in each of the categories you listed in the previous exercise. Some may be at a five on the scale and others may be at an eight or nine. Be very truthful here. It's a checkpoint to anchor you in the reality of where you are now in relation to where you want to be. Do your ratings now. Don't guess. Find out from others if you have to so you have a true, eyes-wide-open understanding of the status. Now take a look. Whatever your scores are on each category, that's where you are now.

QUESTIONS: (These are just some questions to get you started. You can add others.)

- What am I missing?
- How am I feeling as I'm looking at this now?
- Where should my focus be first?
- How would others rate where we are?
- Who else should I share this with to get their input?

Make note of your thoughts.

PICK YOUR PASSENGERS WELL

It's all about fit. Yes, you will need the right skills and competencies in the people you hire. That's a given. What gets glossed over however is the question: Will this person really fit in this role, this team, this culture, in this geography? A few years ago, I was fortunate enough to meet two gentlemen, Adrian Wood and Gerrit Zaayman, who are among the co-founders of a strategic business solution, ShadowmatchUSA, that is based on just this principle: Without the right people in the right roles, achieving your goals can take longer and cost more in the way of dollars and missed opportunities and a dozen other budget- and resource-draining woes. Hiring good people and putting them in the wrong roles has the same effect as hiring bad people. Both will exact damage from your topline and bottom line. Without understanding habits of behavior—yours and theirs—it's hard to get a team to mesh and work productively together. And what if you could benchmark your top performers in each role to understand what makes them top performers? What if you could know this so that you could, as part of your interview process, make sure you were asking the right behavioral questions and, more often than not, select the right person? In his book, *Hiring for Attitude*, Mark Murphy points out that when he conducts certain exercises that identify what makes for a company's low performers, rarely does he ever see that the issues have anything to do skills. As a matter of fact, the maddening part is that the low performer's skills are good; it's their attitude and behaviors that are subpar. Alternatively, when asked to describe their top performers, skills don't rank at the top—attitude and behavioral habits do. The issue here is that it is easier to test for skill than it is for attitude and behavior. That's trickier. Add to that fact that most people are woefully inept at interviewing without bias. Not only that, but as Murphy points out, like I do, the power is in the question and so is the value. If you read Murphy's book and give a call to people at ShadowmatchUSA, you will be armed with what you need to make more of the right choices for the most important reason that will drive whether you achieve or fall short of your financial, customer service, and market share goals: your people. And I'll add one more resource, which is a must read for every senior executive and I'm not talking just HR. I'm talking C-suite. It's a paper by Reid Hoffman, Ben Casnocha, and Chris Yeh called *Tours of Duty: The New Employer/Employee Contract – HBR June 2013*. This paper is groundbreaking, thought-provoking, timely, and relevant. It also is a gear shifting approach and demonstrates how thinking differently about an age-old issue that still challenges us today—staffing and finding the right person for the role—can create some viable solutions.

MIND *SHIFT*

Think about the team you have around you.

- How many of them would you really try to save if they were one foot out the door?

- Who are the top performers in your company?

- Why do you consider them so?

- How does your recruiting process stack up?

- How much have bad hires cost you in the last two years?

Do the math to help make this real for you. Think about the last person you offered a job to. Why did you select that person? Write down the reasons and then score them from 1-5 with 1 = least important and 5 = most important. How did it turn out? Did they live up to the top reasons that convinced you to hire them? What have you learned?

Okay, so you're clear on your why, the purpose that has compelled you to take this journey, and you're clear on your what, that which you wish to achieve and what that desired outcome looks like. You have your team together or are in the process of pulling them together and you've released the brake and are on your way. You will come face to face with wide open roads and a smooth ride and you will also run into various road hazards that will challenge your progress. Here are some well-known ones.

CHAPTER 4

Hazards On the Road

ENCOUNTERING STORMY CONDITIONS

Who likes to encounter bad weather? But what if you could take advantage of adverse forces that you run into? What if you could turn adversity into opportunity or leverage it positively?

Most people don't know how a magnificent animal, the eagle, handles oncoming storms. The eagle's senses, like those of many animals, are alerted when a storm is in its early stages. It hits their internal radar and the eagle begins to respond even before any visible change is evident. What they do is go to the highest point they can find, usually on a mountain. They perch there and, as the winds pick up and atmospheric changes occur, the eagle takes it all in and then an amazing phenomenon happens: the eagle adjusts its feathers so as to use the storm's wind gusts to allow it to fly despite the force of the storm. Think about that. The eagle uses the power of the storm to stay above it and make the most of it instead of just getting blown around or being at the mercy of its force and duration. Readying itself by observing and making adjustments, even minor ones, the eagle is able to make the best of what it cannot stop from happening.

We, more often than not, have no control over the circumstances that blow in and out of our lives. Some people just shrug their shoulders and wait for the inevitable believing that there is nothing they can do about it. Yes, decisions are made without our input, events happen with little warning. Yet we must deal with them as we make our way on the highway toward our destination. We must deal with the storms that rage against all that we've worked for, all we still strive toward, and the values that define us. We must deal with what gets in our way. That's life. Always has been; always will be. The question becomes, how will you choose to handle it? How can you use these times to your advantage like the eagle?

What kind of internal chatter goes off in your brain when you get the first hint of an approaching storm? Do you operate from a place of fear and swoop down to the ground, get the troops fired up, and try to "batten down the hatches," protecting against losses as soon as possible? Do you hunker down and hope it passes over you with the least amount of damage? Do you seek out higher ground to take a look at the entire landscape, considering the big picture and all its options? Do you first try to get a sense of what's going on to get on top of it and ride the most favorable currents? Which of these options do you choose and when? Do you adjust your leadership "feathers" in a way that inspires and shows the way or do they just get ruffled?

MIND *SHIFT*

When "bad weather" is approaching, here are just some questions you should consider:

- Do I/we have clarity about the reality of this situation?

- How can I/we make the best of what's coming this way?

- Is there another way to think about this situation that I/we haven't considered?

- Where is the opportunity here?

- Should I be the one to lead us through this?

- If I am going to lead, how can I best prepare myself to lead the way?

- What will success look like after the storm has passed?

After the storm

- What can I/we learn from how I/we dealt with it?

What storm is approaching for you right now? What are its characteristics? List them here. What meaning are you making of what you've listed? Is it true? What can you leverage about this storm that will help you make the best of it or use some of its power to get you where you want to go?

Make note of your thoughts.

DETOURS—WELCOME THEM

You've embraced the reality that there will be inclement weather along the way and are considering ways to think about how to make the best of them and perhaps even use their power to your advantage.

Now, you see the sign: Detour. Seriously? You're off balance, you didn't plan for this. You're in uncharted territory as you are directed to take another route. With no warning, that which was a clear path is now no longer and you are plunged into a world in which you are a stranger. Your plans seem to blur before your eyes.

But wait, you now have ways of thinking about sudden shifts in the environment and situation. You are beginning to embrace that circumstances often change at will and what you control is how you choose to respond. You are learning not to make decisions out of panic and to let your brain calm down and reframe what is going on. I highly recommend that you watch a wonderful TED Talk called "Living Beyond Limits" by Amy Purdy. (TED Talks are highly engaging inspirational brief presentations by some of the greatest minds in the world covering a wide span of topics. Every leader should put this on their Favorites bar and watch 1 each week. All TED Talks available at www. TED.com) Amy became a professional snowboarder despite losing both her legs and she speaks about taking control of your life and limits. Like Amy, we must decide how we will move on from experiences that we never saw coming—the detours that threaten to steal our success, happiness, and achievements. Or is it the way we choose to think about the detours that is the real thief? Most amazing about this young lady is how, after months of personal implosion and retraction from the world, she emerged, as she puts it in her video, as the author of the new chapter in her life. Listen again closely to the *mind shift* she made and how she chose to see her circumstances—the loss of both legs below her knees, her spleen, one kidney, and the hearing in her left ear due to bacterial meningitis at the age of nineteen. She saw opportunity where some would have seen only boundaries, e.g., "Hey I could pick different length legs so I could be taller or shorter depending on the height of the guy I was dating." Wow! What a way to think of it.

What detours are you encountering in your life that are threatening to get in the way of your progress? What is the story you're attaching to it? Is that story lifting you and others up? Is it the ball and chain that impedes your progress and weighs you down? Do you see only barriers and stop signs?

As leaders, we must shift *our* mental gears first in order to influence our teams to do the same. We have the opportunity to be a beacon of light that shines through the fog and shows the way for how we can deal with losses and sudden redirection on life's road. Great leaders can take this "thing" that has happened and turn it into a runway on which we can accelerate our lives and give our efforts the lift they need to take off.

MIND *SHIFT*

- What opportunities do the detours you are encountering offer you? Name at least three.

- What about the current situation you're facing?

- What detours could you reframe as a springboard to create a better solution?

Note your thoughts.

As Amy Purdy said, "It's not about breaking down borders. It's about pushing off of them and seeing what amazing places they might bring us."

LIMITATIONS: SIX-LANE TRAFFIC ON A TWO-LANE ROAD

I remember a time in my earlier career when I worked as a Sales Director for a leading mortgage banking company. One of our offerings was a mortgage program for our client companies' general employee population. The program was successful. It did, though, have certain limitations that were imposed by our clients: We could never initiate contact to their employees to talk to them about mortgages. The employee had to initiate that call. Additionally, the client would never "endorse" us to their employees. They would only offer it as an option employees could choose if and when they needed a mortgage. It was positioned as a "nice to have" benefit (along with discount tickets to theme parks and the theater) not a "critical need." They also wouldn't spend any money for this marketing. How could we bring this great program to the next level?

When I first joined the division, they had beautiful brochures which our top notch marketing department created and sent out to all employees of each client who agreed to engage in this program. This was done on a schedule about once a year with follow up communication later on if the client agreed to it. As I considered this, I thought, "But everyone isn't ready to finance at the same time of the year when those brochures are sent." The rate environment was highly favorable at this time, and I felt strongly that there was an opportunity here. I asked, "How else can we work with these limitations in a way that hasn't been tried or thought of yet? How can we think about this differently? How can we reposition this program so its value was aligned with other valued, critical needs like healthcare, retirement, tuition reimbursement, and savings programs the companies offered?" (This last question would take too long to share with you so I'll just focus on the first two. This last one though was a key link to shifting the mindset of how our clients saw this program as it related to their employees.)

I asked myself some questions: "What are other ways to communicate with the employees throughout the year? How could we get in front of the employees to be at the point of sale? How could we create leads from that? What if we provided value by educating the employees to become more informed buyers of mortgages so that they had the best chance of making the right decision at the right time for a mortgage?"

Just about that time, a very talented and creative person had joined the already fantastic marketing group and was looking to collaborate with one of the salespeople to develop a presentation around this new interactive technology and use it in the field. I jumped at that.

Together with another wonderful marketing person, we developed a seminar, "Demystifying the Mortgage Process." Then came another limitation from the clients: "You cannot pitch your company to them during this presentation. This must be information only." I said, "Got it. Would you mind though if we got written permission from each seminar attendee to call them as a follow up? We would do this by way of a brief four question survey at the end of the seminar, which we'll hand them and when they fill it out and hand it back, we will give them their smart little desk clock with our name and phone number on it." They liked that approach (I relieved the threat response regarding Fairness and Trust and heightened the reward response toward Autonomy and Certainty) and we had a deal. And thus, for the first time, we had leads coming out of each seminar in the form of those attendees who gave us permission to call them by printing their name and phone number on the survey. These leads went to our call center and they followed up with a call to the attendees.

In the end, we got more business from this process. And we got something more as did the client contact—visibility and image boost. Because these seminars gave our client contacts an unexpected image boost (reward hit to Status) for providing such a useful experience to the employees, they opened the door for us to develop and implement in their companies a more robust and consistent communication plan about this program throughout the year.

What were the original limitations?

- No calls initiated to the employees—no leads to follow up on.

- We had no retail sales force and thus no presence at the street level.

- Limited communication plan throughout the year. Client didn't want to inundate their employees with outside messaging.

- Company would not endorse us to their employees to use us exclusively.

- They would not pay for the marketing for this program

How can you embrace your limitations and use them? For more inspiration, watch the TEDtalk, "Embrace the Shake" by Phil Hansen an artist who challenges us to spark our creativity by thinking "inside the box."

MIND *SHIFT*

Instead of trying to change the limitations, how can you lead the charge with the collaboration from others to embrace the boundaries and work creatively with them?

- What's the story you are telling yourself about the limitations you encounter?

- Are they true?

- How can you take another picture of your situation to see it from a different perspective?

- How can you work more positively and creatively within the limitations that exist?

- What haven't you tried yet?

DEALING WITH ROADBLOCKS

As the saying goes in the Talmud, "We don't see things the way they are. We see things the way we are." I saw this in action when I was in Florida a couple years ago to facilitate a sales strategy retreat for a client. The morning after arriving, I decided to have breakfast at this little local cafe that prominently posted a sign for $3.99 breakfasts. Deal of the century, plus local places are always the best and the crowd they attract usually adds the entertainment factor. So, I took a seat at the bar where you can usually strike up a conversation (or not) with folks. Well, I never found that $3.99 breakfast but as the server placed my bill on the bar, a gentleman took a seat next to me. One look at his eyes and his face and one listen to his voice and I knew I had to hang around a bit.

Immediately, the title of the Ernest Hemingway novel *The Old Man and the Sea* came to mind. As it turned out, he was a seventy-two-year-old man who had sailed around the world twice. He left in 1999 and returned in 2004. His name is Jim. His face was lined with the lasting impressions of years in the sun. The wind and the salty water had left deep trails on his cheeks and around clear blue eyes that seemed to see a horizon that is visible only to those who have traveled alone on the sea.

He told me his story and then he asked if he could share the one truth that guided his interactions with others. My bill laid unpaid on the bar as I leaned in to hear what he had to say. He said, "Well I am a mechanical engineer by trade and I've also worked for companies, started and still have my own company, and picked up and dropped off young people and old people when I sailed around the world. I've been married and divorced. The one thing I've learned is this: *If the resistance is high, the approach is wrong.* Whether I'm working with something mechanical and it won't do what I want it to do, dealing with the force of nature at sea, or whether I'm asking a lady to dance: If the resistance is high, my approach is wrong. I have to shift my thinking and the way I'm coming at it."

Well, that's it isn't it? Boiled down so succinctly into a convenient and useful sound bite. And it's applicable no matter who you are or what your situation is or who you're dealing with. (I asked him if I could quote him at my meeting and his eyes lit up and he smiled as he said, "Would you really? Of course you may.") If the resistance is high, your approach is wrong. If you're the one who wants something from someone else, it is up to you to shift how you're thinking about approaching them. What does this person care about? What is the gap between what I want and what they want? Why should they want to do what I'm asking? What meaning could they be making of my approach? My idea? My request? Take a look at all the conflict we have going on today. What could we accomplish if we weren't so stubbornly tethered to the way we *each* see it? Who could we get on board with us if we just understood how to engage those folks who seem to resist ideas that make so much sense to us—and maybe even to them—but they're still not budging?

Everyone at some point is trying to influence someone to do something they want them to do. Most of us apply the same principle we do when we're trying to speak to someone who doesn't understand us or our language—*we just talk louder.* (Yeah, that usually works.) This is usually followed by trying to bury the person in facts and proof that you're so smart and they just don't get it. Perhaps there's someone else in the conversation that doesn't get it?

The key here is to stop doing what obviously isn't working. Something about your approach needs to change. Press pause. Ego? Check it at the door. If you focus on only one thing starting now, consider this to be it. You will amp your value, success rate, and approachability significantly while lessening your stress level and the need to talk loudly. Don't just take it from me—listen to the old man and the sea.

MIND *SHIFT*

Thinking about your chosen situation that you've taken with you on this journey from the beginning, ask yourself these questions and make note of your answers:

- Where do I have to be with this person?

- What am I not understanding or hearing?

- How does my approach need to shift?

- What does this person care about concerning this issue that I'm not addressing?

- Am I clear about how they're seeing it?

- What is their behavior trying to tell me?

- What is their intention that isn't being fulfilled here?

WARNING: HAZARDOUS SILENCE AHEAD

So, you're still on the road, keeping your destination in mind. Though you've made some progress, you've encountered barriers, been redirected by some detours, encountered some storms, and hit some road blocks. It hasn't been pretty. Now there is a deafening silence in the team broken by the occasional throat clearing. A voice goes off in your head, "What are they thinking? They're thinking I don't know what I'm doing. I'll just shut up and keep driving."

There is truth to the saying, "Silence is golden." As an executive coach, we learn that silence is a very powerful part of communication. This is particularly true when the coach has asked a powerful question and the person needs to process it. Silence is powerful as part of brainstorming and creativity. We don't always have to do everything together in collaboration twenty-four hours a day, seven days a week. Alone time to silently ponder is healthy and needed too.

It's when silence is holding in something that must be spoken and dealt with that you run into trouble. It's the kind of silence that deteriorates relationships and results. When speaking up is seen as a threat to the speaker and the receiver, it can cause catastrophic consequences. Last year, I met with a client of mine who reports to the CEO of a multi-million-dollar, high-profile company. While his situation felt unique to him, it was a very familiar story told by many of my clients. This executive was at that point in his life where he was realizing that the road he was on—which had been a highly successful and lucrative one—was not "filling his bucket." I asked him what he meant by that metaphor. He said simply: "I feel empty and the more I put into my life, the more I feel it draining out the bottom." We continued our dialogue with me asking him challenging questions that probed beneath initial answers. Ultimately what emerged was a pattern of him not communicating his truth professionally and personally. While he essentially loved what he did, his success brought promotions and each promotion inched him a little further away from what genuinely energized him.

I asked, "What is the hard conversation you're not having?" He told me. Then I asked, "So what is making that conversation hard to have in your mind?" And of course it was his perception of what the consequences would be if he spoke his truth—and none of them were good. I then challenged him on his perception, "Is that true?" Silence and then, "No. I really don't know. I'm just imagining." I observed that there were already consequences of not speaking his truth and those are factual. He is living those consequences right now. What he had going on in his head was actually only his own perceptions. How does he know what others will say or how they will respond? Did he become a mind-reader along the way? As we discussed it, he realized that he is in control of how he thinks about and presents his ideas and thoughts and that he had been perceiving (and projecting) the worst outcomes and reactions and making them fact. Then he imagined more awfulness on top of that, which paralyzed him into doing nothing about his situation and sinking further into a life that didn't feel like him. This is typical of our brain's organizing principal that I mentioned in chapter 2 about the SCARF model. Bad is stronger than good, and our tendency is to imagine the worst, which can be useful as part of a larger thinking strategy and habit of mind. It can also be detrimental if it keeps us from the life we should live or the actions we should take.

"What do you want to have happen here?" I asked. He detailed his thoughts and we worked through that. This included clarifying what he really wanted to do going forward with his life and career. Then our focus turned to how he imagined presenting this in a way that would be authentic and also preserve his reputation, relationships, and maybe even his job, if that's what he wanted in the end. I asked him, "What is the best that could happen here?" He said he had an idea of how they could restructure his role to place him right where he wanted to be or if not, he would resign with integrity and with relationships intact and they would be supportive and actually help him in any way they could to achieve his goals. This last part he added with a snort of cynicism.

So the day finally arrived and with a deep intake of breath, he had his hard conversations. He called me later and, with amazement and energy in his voice, recounted the experiences he had, which did end with a huge amount of support, affirmation, and desire for ongoing discussion coming from the very people he feared facing. He did end up leaving and on the best of terms including the opportunity to do consulting work for this company. Most recently, he launched his company and began living into his desired future, which tapped all of his talent and allowed him to operate in his flow and begin to create the life for him and his family that he had imagined. The story is still unfolding and he is now enjoying an already successful ride.

Additionally, the experience helped him realize that not having what he considered to be hard conversations is much worse than what really happened when he had them. In fact, each year, I have some form of this conversation with most of my clients and it always ends up the same: That which they feared did not materialize and actually the opposite did. They had the courage to open that door and step out of the darkness and into the light of truth, which in the end served all. Silence is the debris left by fear. If we can break that silence, we free ourselves from the bonds that keep us from living the life we should and creating the results we can. Is it always easy? No, not always. And neither is living a lie. That's much, much harder and the silence keeps you imprisoned in a cage. The good news is—the cage has a door to which you always have the key to free yourself. If you need more inspiration in this area, try Ash Beckham's TED Talk, "We're All Hiding Something. Let's Find the Courage to Open Up."

MIND *SHIFT*

- In what situations that you are facing now is silence (avoidance) creating chasms of distrust and misunderstanding?

- What is a conversation that you aren't having that you know you should?

- What threats are being triggered when you think about having this conversation?

- What is the outcome of this conversation that you want to move toward?

- How could you reframe the conversation so that you and the other person could see it positively?

Make a commitment today to schedule time to have this conversation. Sit down today and write what stories are keeping you from speaking your truth and liberating yourself and possibly others from the dark place of silence. Make note of your thoughts.

EXERCISE: Create statements that define what you want to do going forward. (It's easy to look back and admonish ourselves for what we didn't do. The thing is it's in the past. Done. No do-overs. Live, learn and move on.) So let's deal in forward thinking based on learning from our past. Here's the framework you can use or create one of your own with the same essence:

The next time _____ (fill in your trigger the keeps you silent.) happens, here's what I will do instead _____

(define it—specifically). Create as many of these as you have triggers for the behaviors you wish to shift that will help you have the conversations you need to have.

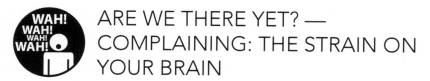

ARE WE THERE YET? — COMPLAINING: THE STRAIN ON YOUR BRAIN

Okay so let's face it, going the distance in achieving goals is not an overnight exercise. Many times, it's a long haul. Remember when you took those trips with your family when you were a kid? Your mom probably packed food and all sorts of games to keep you occupied; perhaps she even made up a few games you could play along the way like finding out-of-state license plates. Then, the inevitable happens—every parent knows this. From the backseat comes the weary voice that can only be mustered from a child bored from being on the road for thirty-five minutes, "Are we there yet?" But they don't stop there. The complaints start to mount. "I'm tired! I'm bored! This is stupid! When are we going to eat? I'm hungry! Suzi's hitting me! Tell her to stop!"

Now I'm sure with little effort you could translate that into the workplace when your team has been working on several projects or initiatives for a while—what does that sound like? "Why are we going in this direction? What's the point? I don't have the budget or resources to make this happen! How many priorities can we have!?! They're not pulling their weight on this project and it's dragging us down." On and on.

Even science proves that listening to negativity is a downer for your brain and anyone else' who hears it. Being surrounded by negative, complaining people is, plainly stated, a bummer. Have you ever noticed how your eyes can start to glaze over when listening to someone spilling out every negative detail of an event or a person? There's a kind of heaviness and dulling out of your mind as you listen to continual complaining. It wears on you and worse, it can suck you down into its whirling vortex of viral toxicity and deaden your best thinking and energy.

Now, when you are going through a really bad time and have had some tragic events happening and you're still working it through, venting about that is different. People don't just "snap out of it". This is real and we all go through it and need good people who will listen and support us to come out the other side. We also need to be that person who will listen to others. It all comes around.

No, I'm talking about destructive and usually, useless, complaining. It is often the same refrain repeated by those who will invest more time in spreading the vitriol than in thinking about what to do about it. They are usually looking to increase their ranks of complainers too. This justifies their choice to continue living in that space rather than making any attempt to take a step in a positive direction—even if that step is just in their mind. Does anyone out there who listens to complainers ever really feel better, more energized, or enlightened afterwards? More so, do the complainers themselves ever really feel better? If they claim to, how long does that "euphoria" last? Be honest.

What complaining actually does most of the time is keep you trapped in a loop of thinking and emotional responses that dumps you where you started—right back in the place where your misery began. Neuroscience tells us that your brain will attend to what you focus it on. The neural wiring will embed more as you continue to "go down that path" of negativity and complaining, reinforcing the stories and patterns of logic (that are usually flawed, one-dimensional, and catastrophized), as well as the emotional responses that accompany this thinking. Much better to use this energy to just acknowledge what is and ask yourself a few questions. Doing this will move you (and anyone within earshot will be grateful) to a more positive part of your brain that has a good chance of solving what you're complaining about or at least help you cope until you do. Shirzad Chamine, who wrote Positive Intelligence, has a wonderful approach around this. He talks about our Saboteurs and Sages and how we need to weaken our Saboteur voices and engage our Sages. Saboteurs are a cast of characters that whisper in our minds messages of judgment, criticism, victim-speak, and

What complaining actually does most of the time is keep you trapped in a loop of thinking and emotional responses that dumps you where you started—right back in the place where your misery began.

more counterproductive chatter that gets us nowhere except on everyone's list of people they want to avoid and further away from reaching our goals..

As a leader, you need to model the way you want others to behave regardless of the circumstances. Have a process by which you regulate your emotions. I don't mean stuff them down—regulate them by dialing them to the *right level* to align with others and channel your emotions into useful action or purpose. When you feel high emotion, try to name your emotion. Then seek to figure out what your emotions are trying to tell you before you express them.

An executive client of mine shared with me during a coaching meeting that she was struggling with the massive change that was coming that was going to highly impact her particular group. She had been with the company a long time. She had roots there and felt very connected to its history and her people and what they built during those years. How she chose to express her passion and emotion around this change was affecting how her manager saw her as a leader and certainly impacted what cues her people took from her to process and respond to what changes were on the horizon. She would have emotional rants occasionally and was seen as resisting certain decisions that were falling into place. Inherently, there is nothing wrong with being passionate about something. It's actually very good and can be powerful—depending on how you channel it. I shared this perspective with her and said that we don't want her to be less passionate. I asked her how she could channel this passion positively that would help the very people whose careers she was concerned about. She thought about that and I heard later on that she spoke at a meeting with the entire staff and did a tremendous job speaking from the heart with authenticity and positivity. Homerun! Look, it's okay to vent. Sometimes we have to do that in the confines of your immediate team or an understanding boss. When you leave the room and walk the halls, however, you need to walk like a leader to model the way and reframe the way you see change positively not only for others but for yourself as well.

MIND *SHIFT*

Catch yourself in the act. (Again I'm not talking about when you really need to just vent or are in tough times and could use a shoulder to lean on and an ear to listen or you are in some serious trouble and need help. Hopefully you can tell the difference by now.)

When you catch yourself spiraling into the complainer abyss, press pause and redirect. Breathe deeply three times. If you meditate, go for it. You only need to do this for about thirty seconds. If you wish to take a longer time, do it. Or go for a short walk and just take in the surroundings. Doing something physical even for a brief time.

Then, ask yourself:

- What is this really about for me?

- Is the meaning I've attached to my complaints really true?

Instead of wishing it were different, or wishing others would be or do something else, try this:

- Accept what is happening (not that it's okay that it's happening, just the reality that it is occurring) and assess it neutrally from a dispassionate distance. Focus on the facts of what is. List them on paper or voice record them.

- What opportunity is this offering me that I didn't have before?

- What do I want to have happen here?

- What can I do to make the best of this?

- How can I make it easier on me and others while we figure out what to do next?

- What is within my sphere of influence and power to change, cope with, or see differently about this situation?

- What do I control here?

- How do I want to feel when dealing with this situation?

- If someone were to catch me on film dealing with this situation, what would make me proud to see?

Here's what I know is within your power: The choice of how to respond to what happens around you.

DEALING WITH UNRULY PASSENGERS

"The best way out is always through."
– ROBERT FROST

Sometimes, you thought you put the right team together and yet some individuals just didn't end up in the right seat. Or they were the right fit for the road you were on but since you had to take some detours and had to make some changes while en route, what you need from them requires a different skillset. It isn't doing them, you or the initiative any good to prolong the agony. And so, you need to deal with it. The first place you have to deal with it though is within yourself.

Isn't it interesting that when things are going wrong, we look externally for the fix-it solution or for the cause of what's gone south? When working with clients, I will often hear phrases like, "When will they listen?"; "What were they thinking?"; "Why don't they get it?"; or "I wish people would just…" When we want change, rarely is our first action to go internal to ask ourselves questions that will reveal new ways of seeing a poor performer. Not that you keep them because you feel sorry for them but that you assess how it came to be and what role you may have in it. Perhaps you thought they were a good fit skill-wise but it turns out attitude and culture—not so much. You ask silently, "Why didn't I see that? Or "Did I see it and ignored my own gut feeling?"

What keeps us from spending time inside our own brains to find solutions and higher awareness? What keeps us from asking, "What role do I have in what is happening now?" What we think is what we do, so it's important to listen carefully to the internal chatter of our minds. Most times, if we introspect about a situation or relationship that's frustrating us, we will find that we have a hand in why it is not where we want it to be.

I worked with Danielle (not her real name), the director of production operations, for a large, national financial institution. She presided over about sixty people.

In our initial discussion, Danielle indicated that she just wished people would behave well and do their jobs. She talked about this small group of people who were just an annoyance and disruptive. She had made a few attempts to get them to change but to no avail. In particular was a person who was the ringleader—Jim (also not his real name)—who was the driver of the disruptive behavior and negative attitude. Now she didn't want to deal with it because she perceived it would cause disharmony and just make things worse. She had made some attempts in the past but never followed through on what she and Jim discussed and he just kept on behaving poorly.

Part of our discussion went like this:

Me: "What are you teaching this person by avoiding dealing with this in a decisive way?"

Danielle: "That it's okay to behave this way. I hate confrontation. I just don't want to make it worse."

Me: "Make what worse?"

Danielle: "His behavior and the effect he has on others and harmony. It would disrupt harmony and I hate confrontation."

Me: "Do you have harmony now?"

Danielle: "No. No I don't actually. (First aha! moment) I really have to deal with this. I just hate confrontation." (Third time she's said this but I'm not going for the bait.)

Me: "And what happens if you deal with this well?

Danielle: "He'll either get his act together or I'll fire him."

Me: "And if he gets his act together or you fire him, what will you have then?"

Danielle: (eyes wide open with a wry laugh) "Peace."

Me: "And what else?"

Danielle: "Harmony—people will get work done in a better way without all his noise and negative impact."

Me: "Fantastic! What else is at risk here if you don't take action?"

Danielle: "Well, the other week, two people came up to me and asked why I am putting up with it. I told them that I just didn't want to make it worse."

Me: "Hearing yourself say that now, what do you think about that statement if you're seeing it from their point of view?"

Danielle: "Cop out. Not a very good manager."

Me: "Is that true?"

Danielle: "With regard to this situation, yes, I have to say it is. I am making him more important than all of them. (Good insight) Actually, I am making my own fear of dealing with him more important than them." (Huge insight)

Me: "Great insight there, Danielle. Way to go."

So we went on to work on how Danielle could find her voice and her strength, how she could reframe what she considered "confrontation" so that she saw it as a conversation that she could be herself in. She realized that she didn't control others' emotions and only controlled her own. She also got out of her office more to be more visible so she could connect more with her people. She did deal with Jim swiftly and in a way that was authentic, clear, and fair with specific measures and dates for follow up, as well as consequences for not meeting the goals set out that showed this person that he had a decision to make. In the end, she did keep him to a set of standards and failing that, she fired him. The response from the rest of the team was very positive and affirming and she learned that everyone wished she had done it sooner. Once she did, her credibility took a leap upwards. This actually catalyzed her to step into her role more assertively, still combining her natural empathy now with confidence and clear guidelines that taught everyone she wasn't a push-over, was fair, and meant what she said. Production metrics improved as did her reputation as a manager, both in operations and with her sales partners. In the end, Danielle realized that the only way out of a bad situation is to go through it and sometimes, it really isn't as bad of a journey as we thought it would be.

MIND *SHIFT*

So now, I want you to think about a situation where you just don't like how other people are behaving or performing. Just pick one. I'm sure you have at least one that is driving you nuts. Now what has been the story you've been telling yourself about it? Typically we ask these kind of questions:

Why do they _____?

What is keeping them from _____?

Where is the sense of _____?

When will they stop _____?

How can they be so _____?

Here are some questions that are about zeroing in on the only thing you control in a situation—you. Instead of asking the previous questions, ask these:

Why do I _____

What is keeping me from _____?

Where is my sense of _____?

When will I stop _____?

How can I be so _____?

Turning these questions around helps to make us accountable first. From there it is important to ask yourself what you can do to begin to turn things around. As Marshall Goldsmith said: "You want change? You go first."

Then it's time to put actions together to deal with an unruly passenger. These are my 4 Cs of having a candid conversation:

Be Candid: Don't hold anything back. You must define the undesired behavior or work output and the impact it's having

Be Clear: Give specifics please about your expectations going forward and consequences for not meeting those expectations. Be clear about the What and the Why. Engage them in the how.

Be Compassionate: Remember "the velvet hammer". You must make a point without leaving a bruise or being disrespectful or demeaning. That will just trigger threat responses in the person that are over the top. Not productive. Doesn't show good character on your part either. Affirm what they do well and challenge them to build on that. Let them know you believe they can turn it around and that it's up to them to make that happen.

Be Collaborative: Engage the person to create ways they will shift their behavior and hold themselves accountable. Don't do all the heavy lifting of the thinking here. They need to take the wheel of their own destiny and accountability to turn their performance around. Ask how you can support them in their efforts without taking over responsibility for them. You own your actions. They own theirs.

WHEN DARKNESS SETS IN

What if you could: Speak confidently and compellingly in front of a large audience and get a standing ovation? Become an avid skydiver? Allow a tarantula to crawl around your hand? What if you could stare down that which you have told yourself for years is not in your wheelhouse, your DNA, on your bucket list (but secretly is), because you fear that if you tried, people would see your flaws, shortcomings and that there's something you don't do well or don't know? (Gasp!) Maybe you create fantastic stories around what you think another's perception of your lack of abilities would be. Perhaps you tell yourself the story that, "Ah, it's not that important anyway. What contribution does it make to society? Got more important fish to fry. Don't have time." The list rolls out across the floor. All these stories have one thing in common: They keep the greatest insights into who you are, and what you're capable of, from ever coming to light in your lifetime. They can keep you from living your best life.

An old friend is what's talking here—persistent, relentless and powerful. And this friend goes by the name of *fear*. Truthfully fear is your friend—up to a point. A wonderful TED Talk on the subject is "Smash Fear, Learn Anything," by productivity guru Tim Ferriss. As he points out, fear can tell you what to avoid or move away from. Our perceived fears become the handlers that control our decisions to try or not try something. These puppeteers pull the strings of our social brain warning us that we will look stupid if we fail. They are masterful at raising up one "horrible" consequence after another. True, there is a reason that this kind of vigilant voice is wired in us to watch out for and have fear of certain situations. This is our emotional brain talking. Our analytical regions that integrate with fear messaging can quickly create any number of rational-sounding reasons not to "go there" when our mind signals: Be Afraid. Be Very Afraid. Now it's true that humans would have perished quickly if we didn't have this kind of neural wiring to guide us away from impending danger. What is also true is that fear can also point you in the direction of exactly where you should move *towards*. Probe with the right questions and soon it will be revealed that cowering in the corner of some flawed rational constructs that are propping up your resistance is fear across any number of dimensions. Flaws might be revealed. Status and key relationships and connections could be compromised. (This again goes back to the SCARF model and the dimensions across which we experience perceived threat or reward.)

If you watched the TED Talk video, Tim talked about his first attempt at dancing when he stepped on his partner's toe with his heel. He said that he was concerned with "her perception of what I'd done and so I left and didn't ever dance again." (Did you catch the key word? Perception. Whose perception really caused him to leave—hers or his?) He also shared that he asks himself a question that helps him push through his perceptions and fears: "What's the worst that could happen?"

I know about this fear thing. It kept me from advancing my growth, my business, my purpose, my value to my clients, and my life's experiences early on. Now for those who know me well, this may come as a shock—so brace yourself. For a very long time, I had a fear of speaking in front of any number of people. I mean abject fear that caused flop sweat, tears, missed opportunities I later regretted, and all manner of awfulness. Then I did a mind-shift once I had a chat with myself about what was really getting in my way. You have to step outside of yourself and be an observer. Drag a chair next to you and put "yourself" in it and talk to the You in the other chair. It's amazing how honest you will be. It's also safe because, well, no one else is really in the room. Doing this allows you to say things out loud and hear it—without consequences. You can also do this by tapping a counselor or coach to guide you through this inquiry and clarifying exercise. You get some outside insight that way too. It's really about disrupting the downward spiral and redirecting to a pathway of thinking toward where you want to go. What was my shift? I turned my perspective inside out and realized that my purpose for wanting to speak to audiences came from making it about wanting to give something of value to others.

So I now love speaking publicly. Love it! I have a point of view that I believe in and I want to get it out there. I have received many affirmations that I am on to something that is timely, relevant, thought provoking and compelling in the way that I present it. I had to disrupt the spiral and redirect my thinking and create a new story. I shifted how I saw speaking and didn't make it about me or being flawless in my delivery or being seen as smart enough, good enough, etc., but about serving others in a valuable, relevant way. I shared my excitement about what I believe and have learned works to help us be better. I imagined the spotlight being on my audience and not on me. They have come to hear me because something about my topic intrigues them, they trust my experience, and whatever I give them will be enough. And it has been enough—every time.

What about those unintended consequences that can unfold as a result of facing your fears: inspiration and influence. You inspire and influence others to make shifts in their lives they may not have otherwise made. You create an environment where catalytic innovation can ignite and grow. You can instill a renewed sense of purpose and resolve in individuals and teams to surmount circumstances and achieve anyway. Some shifts are life-altering. Most of the time, you will never know you've had this influence. Every once in a while though, someone will open themselves to you and share the impact you had on them.

Fear, as it turns out, is a very poor leader. It can be a good advisor, but a poor leader. Courage, on the other hand is a great leader. Courage is what we call on when we feel fear and choose to pursue a path anyway. Courage and sense of purpose are what engage our will to challenge our thinking and our stories so we can make the best of what we don't control. We can step into our best selves to make our best contributions in this life—and perhaps influence and inspire others to do the same.

MIND *SHIFT*

- What story are you telling yourself about something you are you afraid of doing but know you must do or really want to do?

- What is your fear about it?

- Take a look at what you wrote. Is it true? If so, what parts are true?

- What stories are your telling yourself that keep you from pursuing it?

- On a scale of one to ten, how motivated are you to find a way to do this? Same scale: How committed are you? How important is it to you to smash your fear and do this?

- Who can help you?

- What's the first step? Set a date by which you will take this first step.

- Picture yourself having taken your shot at this. What do you see?

- Make a note of what is coming up for you now.

POTHOLES, FLAT TIRES AND RUNNING OUT OF GAS

Sometimes, misfortune seems to "smile" just a wee bit too much in your direction. It's like a storm system that just keeps coming. You have to muscle through it to get where you need to go.

And yet, good can come of it.

Just like making a friend of mistakes, there is opportunity in experiencing adverse conditions and ways to take advantage of "many things going wrong at once" that make you stronger, wiser and able to leap tall buildings in a single bound—only kidding about that last one. Not that I wish long strings of misfortune to befall you, just saying that if you find yourself in the middle of a hailstorm of bad times, hang in there and try to learn what you can. As Winston Churchill said: "If you're going through Hell, keep going." Practicing getting through tough situations develops your brain in ways that smooth sailing and good times won't.

In his book, *How We Decide*, Jonah Lehrer explains that between 1940 and 1990 the percentage of airline crashes attributed to pilot error was stuck at 65 percent even with increased classroom training, mandatory pilot downtime, and other aviation policy "improvements." In the early 1990s this number began to decline for one simple but pivotal reason: the introduction of flight simulators in pilot training. As of 2009, the percentage of crashes due to pilot error declined sharply and steadily from the early 1990s to less than 30 percent, with a 71 percent reduction in the number of accidents caused by poor decision-making. Putting pilots into simulated disasters or mechanical failures or bad weather conditions is more effective at priming their minds to spring into effective action than hearing about it, reading about it, or watching it. There is nothing that makes concepts and new information more brain sticky than actually experiencing it and a simulation comes the closest to that.

I am reminded of a story I was told by a young man who was a Captain in the Air Force.

In addition to simulation training, there is much training that goes on in the actual plane when in the air. Seems during his training, he faced multiple "unfavorable conditions" during every training flight in the air—not just in the simulator. Bad weather, unruly crew, losing oil, flames in the engines, the list went on. It was very frustrating and stressful especially when other peers were seeming to have very smooth flights without a lot of challenges. He longed for just one smooth ride. I listened and then offered him a different way to see it. I said: "You know if I had to pick the pilot I'd fly with on a C-5, I'd pick you hands down. Multiple times, you went up in the air and faced multiple challenges and figured them out firsthand along with your instructor. He kept your hand on the "wheel". You are more prepared now to handle what comes out of left field during a flight than any one who had easy flights with no challenges." Learning by living it develops expertise faster than reading about or listening to someone explain it. He did end up certifying and did well during his years as a pilot for the Air Force successfully handling many inevitable and unpredictable situations he faced on the ground and in the air.

MIND *SHIFT*

- What skills do you need to wire into your mind?

- What simulations should you and your team engage in to prepare you for the road ahead?

- When faced with multiple challenges at once, how would you like to handle them?

Use the following format to list situations in which you want to be able to make a shift for better results.

The next time _____
happens, here's what I want to do instead_____

Practice what you wrote. Look for opportunities to apply your desired thinking and behavior.

CHAPTER 5

Veering Off Course and Finding Your Way Back

IT'S OKAY TO BE LOST

No doubt about it, this is hard for some people—particularly executives who are used to presenting themselves as all-knowing, self-assured, confident, and invulnerable. However, think of all you gain when you simply ask for directions instead of wasting resources, time, and energy backtracking. While there is definitely something to be said for the thrill and value of being lost and figuring your own way out, it's not always in the best interests of the purpose, the team, and the timing— let alone your own career. A wise leader will know this and know when to apply the brakes, pull over, and ask for some guidance. *Remember, a great leader doesn't have to be the one who has all the answers or best ideas; a great leader has to have the smarts to find them and recognize them when they are present.* The best ideas and solutions can come from anywhere and anyone and often do.

Important in this step is who to ask and when. Leadership is also about knowing when to let others lead. Handing over the wheel at the right time to the right person is a big part of productive, wise, mature leadership. Sometimes that person isn't very obvious but if there is one thing that many studies now show, it's that no one comes to work wanting to do a bad job. They want you to see them at their best. They want their shot. Giving people a chance to show you what they've got, whether they are your kids or your team members, will often surprise you in a good way. This shows everyone what kind of leader you are as well. It shows that you trust them enough to give them a shot and let them learn. For you, it means you also have to let go. Not

> *Handing over the wheel at the right time to the right person is a big part of productive, wise, mature leadership.*

disappear and disengage, but after you've been clear about expectations and any parameters, you just let go. Your palms are sweaty now just thinking about letting go, right? Allowing others to build into their careers by taking on new responsibilities and being more visible is how you build a strong bench and a sustainable organization that can withstand the uncertainties of life. Think about your own career trajectory. If you're being honest, you will probably be able to find a time when someone took a chance on you and gave you your shot. How did that feel? What did you think of the person who gave it to you? Can you do this for someone in your life? Make sure they clearly understand the goal or purpose, outline how you wish to be kept in the loop, and remind them that you are available as a sounding board and support. Then step back and truly let go. You will more than likely be pleasantly surprised.

MIND *SHIFT*

- What is it about asking for directions, transferring leadership, or requesting help that gives you pause?

- What is the story you have about asking for help or letting go of "owning it all" as it applies to you?

- With regard to your focus task for this journey, how will you disrupt the familiar story of "I have to do it all" and shift to "Who else can I engage here?"

Make note of your thoughts. Also, list three ways you would benefit from bringing others in to help or share their view?

WRONG WAY? MISTAKES ARE YOUR FRIEND

Most people will not remember how they learned to move as babies. How did we learn if we moved a leg this way and an arm that way we would flip over from our backs to our bellies? Trial and error. How did we learn to grab a spoon, get some food on it, and zero in our on lower face, bending our arm and getting (most) of the food into our mouths? Trial and error. Did we have any embarrassment around missing the mark and having a string of spaghetti draped from our chin to our bib accompanied by a creative smear of sauce down our neck? No. We probably even laughed about it. We really didn't know about failure as an embarrassing thing or good thing. When we didn't get the result we wanted, we tried again.

Fast forward to when you were a kid learning to ride a bicycle. How did that go? Well, there was some phase of getting a feel for balance and making sure you kept your feet on the pedals—pedal forward to move ahead; pedal backwards to stop; keep the wheel straight; shift body weight. Whatever way you were taught, no doubt you fell a lot at first. Eventually you'd only fall now and then. Finally you cut a wobbly path forward without falling and then glided effortlessly. You learned by trial and error. You made mistakes – over and over. There was something else, though, that entered during the learning stage for a lot of kids—the embarrassment of continuing to fail and not get it. Maybe you could hear frustration in your parents' voices? You could see other kids riding easily—why not you? Maybe they laughed at you and left you behind. We learned our first fragile lessons that if we are flawed and can't keep up, we are sometimes left out. We weren't worthy of connection with others. This has to do with our social brain and all the learning that goes with it.

As adults, we applied trial and error to bigger problems. Something else continued to develop too as we got older and moved into adolescence and adulthood: Fear of vulnerability and a need to belong, to be seen as enough. Smart enough, good looking enough, lovable enough, worthy enough, athletic enough, handsome enough, pretty enough, strong enough, thin enough, popular enough, rich enough, etc. A very basic human need is to be connected to others, whether we realize it or not. What makes us unworthy of connection? Allowing others to see our flaws? We make the fatal leap and think to ourselves: "If other people see how scared I actually am, how I often don't know the answer, how long it actually takes me to understand things, they won't want to connect with me or think I'm so smart. If no one wants to connect with me, I will be alone." Brené Brown speaks of this fear in her riveting TED Talk, "The Power of Vulnerability," which has made a huge impact for people who have watched it— some, over and over again I might add.

So what does vulnerability have to do with trial and error? And what does trial and error have to do with effective executive practice and leadership? The error part. If we err, we show our flaws and we see ourselves as vulnerable to how others will see us. Another way to look at it is that by revealing that we can err, we also invite others in to make a contribution and to accept their "flaws" and not go underground to cover them up. As a leader, to show what one doesn't know is a way of showing trust, confidence, and wisdom. It is also a vital way to learn and to figure out the best solutions—it's the way to accelerate learning. The world has become too complex to kid ourselves that any one of us always sees the whole picture and all of its components, understands it and all of its components, and can formulate the best way through it all the time.

Many executives believe they live in an environment where they must have all the answers. That they must be seen as right and sure all the time. Certain personality types live this way and can be seen as intellectually arrogant and as bullies and intimidators to others because of the way they express their points of view—as facts, not merely the way they see it.

It is their belief that no matter how complex the problem is that one is facing, they are sure that the way they see it is right and their solution is the best one to solve it—even if they haven't heard anyone else's thoughts. If they do listen to someone else's opinion, they will tend to interrupt them, shoot the idea down, dismiss it, and seek to dismantle it quickly and with merciless surgical precision. We all know people like this. They operate under the belief that, "A lot more things done around here if people just listened to me and realized I'm right."

Many executives believe they live in an environment where they must have all the answers. That they must be seen as right and sure all the time.

What impact does trying to appear flawless have? We don't take risks. We don't try things that hold the possibility of making us vulnerable and being seen as "not enough"—falling short, as somehow lacking, not what people thought we were. And that will just not do, *right*? We'll be in the "out group." This is the story some high level executives—and really all of us at some point—tell themselves. It is our *perception* which cuts off the possibilities for so much more productivity, workable solutions, and keeping people engaged in the midst of trying times.

So the casualty of the fear of vulnerability is the trial and error process. You may bypass other ideas that seem like risks, avoid meaningful and trusting relationships and sit out opportunities to test your mettle.

As a leader and executive, it is important to be decisive for sure. You can't always have a conversation to find out everyone's idea when the bullets are flying. You, as the leader, have to make a decision quickly sometimes. The question becomes how and when that talent for decisiveness is expressed. If a person isolates themselves and makes unilateral decisions alone without engaging others when it is possible and appropriate to do so, he or she runs the risk of teaching their team and those above them any one or more of the following about themselves: a) they don't trust anyone else's thought process; b) they are afraid of being "outsmarted"; c) they don't want input (and then these are the same people who wonder why their staff doesn't come to them with ideas or make decisions on their own); d) they will humiliate anyone who dares to engage in a debate, which these types are usually quite adept at executing; e) they lack confidence in themselves; f) they're not building their team's bench strength and leaving the organization vulnerable. What are you teaching others about your relationship with risk, failure and making mistakes? How could that be affecting your team's performance and behavior?

MIND *SHIFT*

Regarding the issue you selected to focus on in the beginning of this book:

- Where are you feeling lost?

- How is that feeling driving your behavior and thinking about the situation?

- What are you hesitant to try?

- What's the opportunity that being lost is presenting to you?

- Where do you feel vulnerable?

- What impact is this having on your team and progress?

- How can you reframe the internal chatter that is keeping you from allowing yourself to be lost?

- What or who would be helpful to you right now?

Make note of your thoughts now.

KNOWING WHEN TO TAKE THE NEXT EXIT

Sometimes you are driving along a stretch of road, confident that all is well. But gradually, you get that sneaking feeling that something is off. This is usually followed by the unavoidable realization that you are going in the wrong direction. If that thought is running through your mind, chances are good that others traveling with you are having the same thought. Chances are also fairly good that no one is daring to tell you that depending on what their relationship to you is and the level of safety they feel in telling you this. If they are bold enough and confident enough to do so, you will probably experience some level of hit to your Status. This could trigger the: "I'm no quitter! We just have to hang in there a little longer." Or "Hey, I've been down this road before. I know what I'm doing!" Yet, making its way from your right brain to the front and center of your mind is another voice trying to get through: "Uh, excuse me, but you need to turn back. The results are in: The others are right. You're going in the wrong direction." Cue the shoulder slump and the exhaled sigh of dread—maybe even a mix of anger, denial, and certainty that *they* are all wrong and perhaps a heapin' helpin' of judgment of yourself for not knowing better. All of those emotions (and resulting behavior) have to do with anxiety of what you may lose if they're right.

Now look, sometimes you are the lone voice of reason and you are right. It's a matter of having awareness in the moment and mental agility to step back and ask the right questions. Remember, the power is in the questions you ask yourself in time. If you can reframe this kind of awakening—that maybe you are heading in the wrong direction—you can actually turn it to your advantage and make an even better outcome happen.

There are some brain games at work here when you get the sense that you've made a bad decision after you've invested time, money, or energy—not only yours but that of others. One of those games is loss aversion and it is played out on the mental game board based on the theory of "sunk costs." This is the theory that speaks to the situation where you've expended resources that are unrecoverable in pursuit of a goal. It gets triggered when you realize your investment is not going to pay off. You say: "But I've gone this far, just a little more and we'll get there. Otherwise if I quit now, I'll lose what I've put in." Yes, that is true. What else is true is that sometimes, it pays off *bigger* to be a quitter. To take the next exit and get off the road you're on, putting a lid on any further loss. You see, there has to be a shift in the way you see the realization of a bad decision. Continuing to input resources is a *loss* if you continue toward something that is clearly not working. Continuing to input resources is an *investment* if you are putting resources toward a better solution and getting a return. There is also another shadowy voice whispering an ugly threat: "If I admit I'm wrong, I will lose face and also the credibility and trust from my team. What will others think of me?" This is another perceived threat that will keep many a leader from cutting their losses, learning from the mistake, and engaging the team to find a better solution. Showing that no one gets it right all the time and trusting your team to help figure it out, when done with confidence and positive attitude, will be what sticks in people's minds about a leader more often than not. What we focus on—good or bad—is a mental habit. The good news is habits can change.

We are taught not to be a quitter and there are many famous quotes about that. Certainly there are times when you just shouldn't give up—you have to dig deep and find the strength of mind and spirit to continue on. There are other times when it is not only appropriate, but advisable, to quit and to find the nearest exit. Quitting and redirecting thinking, resources, and energies can *actually* avoid continued losses and realize the most gains as opposed to focusing on avoiding *perceived losses* and missing the highest gains.

MIND *SHIFT*

Think of the situation you are facing where you sense you might be in the wrong direction. If you are already down a road and it's not working as well as it should, ask yourself these questions:

- What is keeping you on that road?
- If you stay your current course, how will it pay off? On a scale of one to ten, how likely is it that it will pay off as much as you need it to?
- What is driving you to hang on to something that is not working?
- When you think about discontinuing your current course, what thoughts come up for you?
- How do you feel when you think those thoughts?
- If you are trying to choose between two options, what are you spending the most time thinking about—gains or losses?
- How would you describe your current mindset regarding this situation: Trying to avoid losses (what you don't want to lose or fail at) or seeking to move toward gains (what you actually want to achieve)? Listen to your internal chatter and how you externally talk about it with others?
- What's the next action you want to take?

Make note of your thoughts now.

SECTION
THREE

The Drive for Better Results Never Ends

You made it. Now what? Get on the road again. But before you do that, make a pit stop to do the following:

First, it is time to acknowledge the accomplishment and more important, how you got there. What were the lessons from the road that you can pack in your mind for your next trip? It is a time for thankfulness, gratefulness, and to recognize special accomplishments of the team members. A gracious leader does this.

CHAPTER SIX

Lessons from the Road

YOU ARE THERE

From here, the journey is really about continuing to practice the mind shifting approaches you have learned in this book. Remember, the power is in the questions you ask yourself, your willingness to have your thinking challenged not only by the questions you ask yourself but by those asked by others.

Invite uncertainty to take a seat as one of your road trip passengers. Not always being able to predict does trigger some threat—but some threat is good. It can be a springboard for more creative thinking that comes from other regions of your brain that have been relegated to the trunk and locked up by the one in the driver seat: logic. Let logic and creativity sit side-by-side. Let vulnerability and untested options travel some of the distance with you. Smile when you see detour signs and roadblocks because you, at some point, will need all of them to reach your highest potential and solve the most complex challenges. The gift of getting lost or taking the road less traveled is that those diversions might take your thinking to the very place you need to go.

Now wait, there's a sign up ahead. It says Caution. This sign means to be aware of things that may or may not be seen. When you develop a positive way of moving through challenges, change and crises, when you begin to operate in a world of possibilities when others only see barriers, when you have a great idea that you believe in and are doubling down on, there may be others who will militate against you and try to make you feel foolish for believing in such a "fantasy". In the extreme, they want you to fail. Here's an idea to keep in mind if you run across these types on the road to your destination.

Let logic and creativity sit side-by-side. Let vulnerability and untested options travel some of the distance with you.

I.D.E.A.

I remember back in 2008, a colleague of mine who has a sales training and consulting firm said 2008 was a fantastic year.

A business owner I heard talking to her friend at the Post Office said 2008 was her best year ever.

Wait, are they talking about that year? The year that saw the mortgage industry blow up like Mount St. Helens, stock prices fall, businesses close, and unemployment rise? Seriously? Who are these people anyway?

They are individuals who were exposed to the same events as everyone else but did something different than most: they thought about and focused on opportunities rather than obstacles. They didn't let circumstances dictate their next move and they didn't become victimized by all of it. People who succeed and thrive in a down market choose to focus on what they do control—their own thinking—instead of on what they don't control—the circumstances. Worrying takes you in circles and dumps you back where you started; thinking moves you forward. Those who are creating wealth and success regardless of circumstances imagine alternatives, dare to shift gears, and push through fear. They expect to achieve—and most importantly, act with intention to achieve—their goals. That's the IDEA I'd like to offer you to engage with your own thinking and influence your teams to do the same.

Imagine – Dare – Expect – Act

Here are four steps to setting the stage for moving beyond what you think is possible (and silencing those doubters for good).

Imagine. Set a course. Like Donald Trump says, "If you're going to be thinking anyway, think big!" See your destination as if it's already there. As you did in Section 2, define it, write it down, draw a picture, record your voice talking about it. Make it real. Notice what you're feeling as you're creating the vision of where you want to take your life, your career, your organization, your team. Break it down into phases of achievement so you can see the roadmap to your destination. Do this alone and/or as a team.

Dare. This is where you have to be strong. You will eventually hear it from others: "Can't be done." "You're nuts." "Yeah, good luck with that." "Bad timing." Thank them for their input and then forget it. You must push through the voice that says, "It's never going to work." Courage is having fear about doing something and doing it anyway. Defy the experts and the odds—believe it anyway. Remember, people who don't have the courage to step out and take a risk in order to get what they want sometimes don't like to see anyone prove that it can be done. Surround yourself with people who will encourage you and be good sounding boards who will challenge your ideas and strategies in the spirit of wanting you to succeed. Distance yourself from toxic people.

Expect. Yes, expect that you will succeed. Don't just go through the motions. If you don't really expect to make it, don't bother. Move through your life and decisions with intention. This is where you have to pay attention to the "inner chatter" that's going on in your head as you make your plans and present yourself to others in the pursuit of your goals. What story are you telling yourself about what you want to achieve? Sometimes people technically do the things they're supposed to but when you don't expect to win or achieve your goal, there are a thousand small strokes you will not do and others will feel your lack of authenticity around your actions—and so will you. Many people I know live by the belief of expecting the worst. Why? Here's their answer: "So I won't be disappointed if it doesn't happen." Really? What a horrible way to live and certainly no way to lead. This is the story heard from people who haven't developed an ability to reframe failure and mistakes in a more useful way. It's okay to talk about what could go wrong because that spawns ideas too and ways to prepare and perhaps even some innovative ideas for other businesses. But to go through actions expecting the worst is like marrying someone and making them agree to terms of a divorce prior to getting married. What's the point of walking down the aisle then?

Act. All the imagining, daring, and expecting in the world will not get the results you want. You must take action and the best way to do that is to set intermediate goals to be achieved. Knowing yourself as you do, what approach works best for you to get tasks accomplished? Whatever is most effective, put it into practice now. Work with someone you trust and who will commit to checking in with you to make sure you're staying on track. Taking action is what makes you get real about your dreams and what it will take to achieve them. The Imagining, Daring, and Expecting are like a plane gaining speed and momentum as it accelerates down the runway. Taking action will be what will make all those efforts and your ideas take off and ultimately arrive at the destination of your success.

While much focus is being given to what is bad in the world right now, it is negative and fear-based thinking in response to that news that is making it worse. You tell yourself a story enough times—you start believing it and start living it. The stories that you tell yourself can work against you, or for you, as in the case of Wilma Rudolph.

She was a great Olympic track and field athlete and her story underscores how the stories we tell ourselves and what we make of the circumstances that befall us can change the course of our lives and fly in the face of expert knowledge.

Here are the facts about Rudolph:

- Born prematurely in 1940, the twentieth of twenty-two children. Not expected to survive but did.

- Contracted scarlet fever and double pneumonia at age four. Survived but left leg was paralyzed.

- Took her leg braces off at age nine because she

imagined, dared, and expected to not just walk, but run. Doctors said she wouldn't ever walk again. Her mother thought differently. Rudolph chose to believe her mother.

- She took action and began to exercise and with determination defied the experts.

- By 1956, Wilma Rudolph had an Olympic bronze medal and by 1960 had three Olympic gold medals.

Was it an easy road to reach her goal? No. Was it tough going at times? Yes. Was it worth it? Absolutely.

MIND *SHIFT*

- How can you put this I.D.E.A. into action starting today?

- What are some lessons from a recent road trip that you and your team have taken that you want to remember?

- How will you incorporate them into your thinking the next time you hit the road?

Make note of your thoughts.

CHAPTER SEVEN

Afterword

Okay, I admit to a repeating theme in all the chapters:

Success and creating the life you want is not about *(fill in the blank)*; it's about how you choose to think about *(what you filled in the blank with)*.

The best place to begin when you're going around in loops is at the highest level: Your thinking and your vision. Asking questions like: What do I want to have happen here? What is the outcome I'd like to create or see happen? Making sure you have clarity about a defined purpose is key. Why? So that you can begin to make the best choices as to how to best get there. If you don't define your vision or purpose that is bigger than you, then you are stuck with only dealing in the here and now. You are at the mercy of whatever happens minute to minute. You are making decisions to get through the moment with no attachment to an overarching direction or goal. This is what makes the here and now hard to find your way through. Because people perceive that change and what it might bring will be hard, they often stay the course and stick "with the devil they know" rather than risk tangling with "the devil they don't know". The thing is when people tell me that they're afraid of what might happen or that it seems hard, I ask them: "Isn't what you're going through now hard?" They'll respond 100 percent of the time with a yes. So let me share a thought with you: If you're going to do "hard" you might as well do hard while taking steps toward a life you want. Otherwise, you're doing "hard" staying where you are and just going around in circles of misery getting no closer to where you really want to be.

When your purpose is defined in your mind and you've colored it in with some detail and you've actually visualized yourself "there"—how it will feel, how it will be for you and others—it gives you the fuel and resilience to focus on the challenge in front of you and deal with it because you know it will get you closer to what you want to achieve. You can bring that vision and all the emotion you attach to achieving it into your thinking to make the most of day-to-day opportunities to take yet another step toward that goal. With a positive perspective you can deal with setbacks, pain and missteps and still not lose your footing. Will it always work out in your favor 100 percent of the time just the way you want? No, but the chances are more in your favor if you choose to ignite the best thinking in you.

The power is in the questions you ask yourself. I've offered you many throughout the chapters. Make a list of the ones that resonate with you the most and keep it in your hand held device, under your blotter or in a desk drawer. Make the best one or two a screensaver—whatever will keep them top of mind. Read them every day or just when you need it. Get those questions in your bones. Hardwire them. The theme of the questions, which I'm sure you've grasped at this point, is to challenge your stories that you accept as fact. Take a dispassionate look at the stories you rattle off without even thinking and ask the powerful question: "Is it true?"

Take a dispassionate look at the stories you rattle off without even thinking and ask the powerful question: "Is it true?"

Dealing with obstacles—whether they visit us suddenly or we see them coming a mile away—is inevitable, as is enjoying good times. What you do with them is what counts and influences what happens next. I don't believe anyone has a good time staying in a state of fear. It's exhausting for any living entity. At some point, we humans either give up mentally and physically or find a way to hang in there by changing the mantra in our minds which can fuel our physical and mental strength to carry us forward. Building this habit of mind can last a lifetime. You can build positive and fulfilling experiences even in times of trouble. Yes, you will still feel pain, disappointment and sorrow. We humans are made to feel the full spectrum. What we do with that can be developed. Where we dwell the most, can be shaped. We can evolve into the person we wish to become.

Which brings me to giving you the post-script on "Tommy" and where he is today.

Tommy did keep his promise to his parents and completed his GED when he returned from the war. He then went on to study at the Art Students League in NYC. He married a fantastic lady, Diana Kutchukian, in 1952 and they had two children. He was an advertising executive for top houses in NYC, Grey and Ted Bates, finishing off his career with a packaging design firm, Gaylord Adams/Don Flock & Associates, where he enjoyed a productive and fulfilling career until his retirement at seventy.

Today, Karnig Thomasian, a.k.a. Tommy, is ninety-one years-old and living in New Jersey. His dear wife, Diana, died in 2011. He misses her deeply still. He moved from the home where they lived for more than fifty years and raised a family, to an active independent living community. It

Karnig "Tommy" today.

was there in the spring of 2013, that he had the good fortune to meet a wonderful woman living in the same complex and they fell in love. He built a great life that has been full, adventurous, and generous and he is still going strong. His experience as a POW gave him perspective and allowed him to see adversity and challenges as catalysts for thinking differently. Over the time I've known him, I've learned that his first instinct after recovering from any "initial impact" is to think, "Well, how can I make the best of this?"; "How else can I see this?"; "How can I make this work where I am with what I've got?" It's amazing how much he can make happen with this kind of mental agility when everyone else says it can't be done. He influences action with his positivity and creative thinking in the presence of forces that work against him. Does he always win? No. But he learns and manages to build great relationships along the way. He believes that no matter where you are in life and what endings you've had to deal with, there can always be new beginnings.

I have learned also that among his many attributes that separate him from most, he is a fantastic portrait artist whose charcoal renderings are often mistaken for actual photographs. Karnig infuses each day with hearty laughter,

Karnig "Tommy" with the author 2015

being with friends (and making new ones) and working on many projects at the same time. He loves to play games, build things with his hands and is full of love for his family and his country. He is known as a great friend who speaks frankly, is a generous soul, a great patriot, and a supporter of all veterans from all wars. Most of all, he is the greatest father in the world. I ought to know.

He's my Dad.

APPENDIX A

About the Author

 After over twenty years in the corporate arena, Karla Robertson started her own company, Shifting Gears Business Coaching & Consulting, in 1999. She hosted her own internet-based talk show, *The Exceleration Zone* in 2004 and has been quoted in *The New York Times*, MSNBC Online, and other Internet and national print publications. Karla is also a powerful speaker, igniting the minds of her audiences to challenge their thinking to rise above circumstances and achieve their goals.

Prior to that, Karla was a Marketing Director and the leading sales producer in the mortgage banking industry and a VP of Sales and leading producer in the healthcare industry.

She is a past board member of the ICF-NJ, the state chapter for the International Coaches Association. She has been a volunteer Wish Grantor for Make-A-Wish Foundation of NJ for the past 13 years and continues to help fulfill the wishes of children with life-threatening illnesses. She also serves on their Program Services Committee.

APPENDIX B:

Acknowledgements

To my Mom: a woman with a courageous heart who was a highly adaptable and agile thinker. She was a copious idea-generator and compelling writer. She never met a stranger. She made dinner time interesting as you never knew who would be breaking bread with you. She taught me about generosity, fearlessness and endurance. She also loved to have fun, throw parties with my Dad, tell great stories and jokes and break the rules-which included dancing on tables in a Greek restaurant. There was never a challenge she didn't rise to including the ones that eventually robbed her of her physical strength and sharp mind. She was interesting because she was interested. Her curious nature made her brilliant in any conversation. Because of both of my incredible parents, I am the person I am. Mom shaped the woman I am with her unconditional love, wisdom and belief in all that I am and all I am yet to become. I love you mom and am sure you are up there sharing your best jokes with God.

To my Dad: a man with a generous and loving heart with whom I spent many precious hours. Growing up, some of my most memorable and bonding times were when we actually said nothing as he scanned all the possible things he could do in the massive garage full of his "projects in progress". He would whistle some nameless tune and I would putter with him and stoke the pot-bellied "stove" to keep the garage warm in the winter. Dad is a great friend to all. He has a heart that beats with love, a child-like appetite for fun, and is a devious card player. He is open to new experiences and he is brave in the face of adversity. He has great endurance for tough times and manages to always try to see the upside. Dad, you, along with mom, have been my greatest champions and believers and I will always be grateful for your presence in my life.

To my sister, Linda: who had the resolve and courage to become a single mom at the age of 42, adopting a baby, Alicia, who has grown into a smart, insightful, compassionate and beautiful young lady I am privileged to call my niece. Linda, you are a talented, gutsy, compassionate person and a beacon of hope and love to the children whose lives you touch every day as a teacher's assistant. You're amazing. If

I can have at least half the impact on the lives that I touch through my work as you've made on those children, mine will be a life well-lived.

To my niece, Alicia, who came from far away and yet seems like she has always been with us. I love you for who you are now and growing to be. You are a strong young lady and your spirit and sensitivity to others will serve you well in life.

To my husband David, for cheering me on and making sure I peeled myself away from my computer to refresh and take breaks from the intensity of writing a book. Who cooked dinners and took care of other household duties while I was glued to my computer and who always "keeps the light on for me." I also want to acknowledge him for one of his fantastic sermons that ignited the spark in my mind for the section on Imagine – Dare – Expect –Act.

To my step-daughter Suzi: who fought the good fight and at such a young age showed dignity, courage and spirit right to the end. I love you for who you were and still are in my heart. I feel your presence with me when I need that extra strength to see something through.

To my step-son, Matthew: who I thank for having served his country and for the way he watches over those who are closest to him, most notably as a wonderful dad to his daughter, Emma.

To our granddaughter, Emma: who shows strength, perseverance, love and sweetness each day. You amaze me, sweetheart.

I would like to send a huge hug of gratitude to my core "tribe" who have been by my side listening to the ups and downs of being a business owner with a dream as well as providing encouragement and support along the sometimes lonely road of entrepreneurism. You've listened to my ideas, my pursuits, my challenges and celebrated my successes and joys while at times providing your insights and counsel: Maria (FAB), Catherine, Valerie—many thanks for your thoughts on the manuscript—Donna, Sara, Carmelina, David, Eric, and Josh—thank you for cheering me on and listening to the steps of this journey.

I also want to extend my deep gratitude to all of my clients who have placed their trust in me to walk with them along certain stretches of their life's road when they felt they could use a confidante, collaborator, challenger and someone to give them the straight shot. I know that takes courage and vulnerability along with a desire to create and live into a vision they have for themselves. I also want to acknowledge those clients with whom I have enjoyed continuing relationships that have included referrals to their colleagues, ongoing dialog and in some cases wonderful friendships. Because of all of you, I am able to write this book and live into my vision and purpose for my life to keep growing, serving and dreaming of what comes next. Thank you.

A special shout out to Marsha who shared insights on the manuscript when I needed some feedback at the last minute.

To Jamie Sussel Turner, author of Less Stress Business. Thank you for being my mentor on this road of being a first time author.

To Mary Ellen and Stacey at The Write Room for your initial thoughts and suggestions.

I want to thank those brilliant thinkers out there who have inspired me, taught me and shared their work and research which have influenced me and provoked my thinking about how I can best serve my clients as a coach, in particular: David Rock, Marshall Goldsmith, Carol Dweck, Shirzad Chamine, Daniel Pink and many others.

And finally, to Henry DeVries and his team at Indie Books International for their assistance in helping make this book a reality.

APPENDIX C

Services Available

Karla Robertson integrates in her coaching approach the insights from neuroscience with the inquiry and observation of coaching methodology. She works with C-level executives, other senior leaders, and their teams in organizations across diverse industries and geographies facilitating retreats, providing one-on-one coaching and team development coaching

As a keynote speaker, Karla delivers relevant and thought-provoking talks that challenge how people think and encourage them to develop agility and nimbleness in themselves and their teams. She believes this is the foundation that must be developed now to effectively prepare our minds to deal with the increasing velocity and uncertainty of change and enable us to adapt and flow to create the best outcomes.

KEYNOTES

The Agile Minded Executive: Drive better results by shifting how you think

Where Eagles Dare: Adjusting your leadership outlook to harness the power of any storm

What Was I Thinking?: Shift the stories that are sabotaging your career

Victor/Victorious: Rise above circumstances to make the best of what is

I Got My Seat At The Table. Now What?: Building presence and influence in the executive suite

Visit: www.ShiftingGears.biz

Connect: http://www.linkedin/karlarobertsoncoach

Follow: http://www.twitter.com/thebraincoach

Subscribe: http://www.karlarobertson.com/subscribe/

APPENDIX D

Resources

BOOKS

Jonah Lehrer, *How We Decide, 2009*

Marshall Goldsmith, *What Got You Here Won't Get You There, 2007*

David Rock, Ph.D., *Quiet Leadership, 2006*

Shirzad Chamine, *Positive Intelligence, 2012*

Karnig Thomasian, *And Then There Were Six, 2004*

Daniel Pink, *A Whole New Mind, 2005*

John C. Miller, *QBQ! The Question Behind the Question, 2001*

Dan Heath and Chip Heath, *Switch: How to Change Things When Change Is Hard, 2010*

Viktor Frankl, *Man's Search For Meaning, 1959*

Mark Murphy, *Hiring for Attitude, 2012*

Carol Dweck, *Mindset: The New Psychology of Success*, 2006

TEDTALKS FROM WWW.TED.COM

Brene Brown
Tim Ferriss
Phil Hansen
Amy Purdy
Ash Beckham
Tim Harford

PAPERS/ARTICLES

David Rock, Ph.D., *SCARF: A brain-based model for collaborating with and influencing others.* NeuroLeadership Journal; Issue One 2008

Reid Hoffman, Ben Casnocha, and Chris Yeh, *Tours of Duty: The New Employer/Employee Contract – HBR June 2013*

OTHER

Shadowmatchusa –www.shadowmatchusa.com – Gerrit Zaayman

INDEX

Index words and phrases
4Cs, 80
Agile – 15, 18,22, 23, 41,
Brain
     whole brain, vii
     gift , x
     input from various regions, 18
     brain sticky, 19
     key points, 23-32
     preloading, 39-40
     Where am I?, 43
     Internal chatter, 50
     Calm down, 53
     Negativity, 69
     Focus, 70-71
     Social, 82; 95
     Practicing, 87
     Right brain, 100
     Games at work in, 101
     Creative thinking, 110
Candid conversation, 80

Carol Dweck, 32

Circumstances

    How we choose to think about them, vii-viii, 1

    Tommy's story, 10 – 13

    That you did not create, 21

    Three things that you need, 22

    No control, 22; 50

    Change often, 52

    Inspiring others, 85

Complaining, 68-69; 71

Command and control, 15

Courage- 16, 22, 33, 66, 67, 85, 110

Daniel Pink, 24

David Rock, 29

Detours, 52-54, 63, 75

Eagle, 49-50

Fear

    Not provoke, ix

    Enemy, 9

    Victimized by, 13

    Dial down, 31

    Perceived, 33; 66

    Operate from a place of, 50

    Danielle's story, 78

    When Darkness Sets In, 81

    Of vulnerability, 95

    Casualty of, 97

State of, 117

Growth mindset, 32-33

Gut feeling, 75

Hardwire, 28; 31

    Questions, 117

Hire for Attitude, 45

IDEA, 109-111, 113

Is it true?, 52, 86, 117

Limitations, 55-57

Marshall Goldsmith, 20; 80

Mental agility, 21-22; 35; 100; 119

Mistakes, 61

Old Man and the Sea, 60

Perception, 64, 81, 83, 97

Pilot, 87-89

Positive intelligence, 71

Practice, 40

Speaking (up)

    From the heart, 72

    In public, 84

    When seen as a threat, 63-64

Truth, 67

Questions, ix

    Building mental agility begins with, x-xi

    Tommy's Story, 6, 10

    Challenge thinking, 17

    Power of, 21; 22-23; 42

From threat triggers, 30

Prime mental gears with, 35

Best decision-making begins with, 37

Behavioral, 45

When bad weather strikes, 51

Dealing with limitations, 56

Go internal to ask, 75

Candid conversation, 79-80

Probing to uncover fear, 83

Quitting, 64-65

Resistance is high, approach is wrong, 60

Reward, 21, 28-31, 83

Roadblocks, 59

Saboteurs, 71

Sages, 71

SCARF, 29; 65; 83

Shadowmatch, 45-46

Silence, 63-67

Simulation, 88, 89

Stormy conditions, 49

Team, 91, 92, 98 , 99

TedTalks

Brene Brown, 95

Tim Ferris, 82

Ash Beckham, 67

Amy Purdy, 53

Phil Hansen, 58

Threat, 63

    To speaking your truth, 67

    Candid conversation, 81

Tommy's Story, 3

Tours of duty, 46

Vulnerability

    Executives feel, 20

    Trial and error, 95-97

    Traveling with you, 107

Wilma Rudolph, 112-113